African Studies in the United States
A Perspective

African Studies in the United States
A Perspective

Jane I. Guyer

Director, Program of African Studies
Northwestern University

With the help of Akbar M. Virmani and Amanda Kemp

Library of Congress Cataloging-in-Publication Data

Guyer, Jane I.
    African studies in the United States a perspective / Jane I. Guyer ; with the
help of Akbar M. Virmani and Amanda Kemp.
        p. cm.
    Includes bibliographical references.
    ISBN 0-918456-76-2 (pbk.)
        1. Africa, Sub-Saharan—Study and teaching (Higher)—United States. I.
African Studies Association. II. Title.
DT19.8.G89 1996   96-12430
967'.0071'173—dc20   CIP

Printed in the United States of America

CONTENTS

LIST OF TABLES

Preface - African Studies Association

In recent years, a combination of circumstances has challenged scholars in African Studies to rethink our priorities and premises. With the end of the Cold War, government funding for international projects has been reduced and foundation priorities have turned from area studies to other ways of organizing knowledge. As a result of these developments, the African continent risks becoming increasingly marginalized in academic life.

Given this political and intellectual climate, the African Studies Association is pleased to cooperate with the Ford Foundation to make this report as widely available as possible. Although the opinions expressed are strictly those of the author, the Board of Directors of the ASA hopes that her astute assessment of the field will stimulate the discussion and debate necessary to chart new directions for African Studies in the twenty-first century.

Iris Berger, President
Goran Hyden, Past President
Gwendolyn Mikell, Vice President

Preface - Ford Foundation

The Ford Foundation's interest in African Studies dates from the early 1950's and its commitment to foreign area studies following World War II and the onset of the Cold War. Responding to the need to increase the national capacity to understand other parts of the world, the Foundation supported graduate fellowships for training and field research, in Africa among other regions; contributing to building centers of African Studies at a number of universities throughout the United States; and provided support to key organizations serving the field, notably the African Studies Association and the Joint Committee on African Studies of the Social Science Research Council and the American Council of Learned Societies. In an effort to assist in diversifying the field, through the decade of the 1970's, the Foundation funded the Middle East and Africa Field Research Program for Afro-Americans.

Though general support for area studies has been substantially reduced since the late 1970's, the Foundation maintains several field offices on the African continent, and its interest in Africa remains strong. In recent years, Foundation staff have watched with growing concern the increasing marginalization of Africa in the policy community and among the wider public. The parallel concern relates to the health of African Studies within the academic community, particularly in light of cuts in federal funding. As one way to address these concerns, last year the Foundation asked Jane Guyer, Director of the Program of African Studies and Professor of Anthropology at Northwestern University, to assess the present state of the African Studies enterprise in the U.S., the problems it faces, and its prospects for the future. The quality of the report, together with the numerous requests the Foundation has received for it, persuaded us that it should be made more widely available. The Foundation is pleased to join with the African Studies Association in publishing Professor Guyer's report.

Alison R. Bernstein, Director, Education and Culture Program
Sheila Biddle, Program Officer, Education and Culture Program
Timothy Bork, Director, Africa and Middle East Programs

An overview of African Studies composed at the present moment necessarily represents the perspective of the author, and for two reasons. The study of Africa has become widespread and varied, and therefore may look quite different from different vantage points. And like much else in the present political and intellectual world, it stands at the watershed created by the simultaneous fall of the Berlin Wall and the rise of communications technology. The nature of the vistas beyond is still a matter of intense debate and experimentation. As I moved further into the work for this report, and discovered unforeseen fields of endeavor and ever-ramifying complexities in their achievements, it seemed increasingly preferable to take up the challenge of a necessarily personal view in an explicit fashion, rather than to agonize over or try to neutralize it.

We are at the beginning of a new era in African Studies in this country. There have been two more-or-less marked previous eras, each of which produced a characteristic scholarship that grew out of its own configuration of conditions and concerns. The first was led by a basic research agenda, and grew out of the post-World War II concern with internationalism and the need to have U.S. knowledge about, and a U.S. presence in, the context of the Cold War. In the public view, the struggles for independence and growth were in the foreground. The second joined and changed the first, but did not displace it. It was oriented towards a development agenda, growing most strongly after the Sahelian and Ethiopian famines of the 1970s and early 1980s, and the changed international economic conditions after the collapse of the Bretton Woods agreement (1973) and the rise in world oil prices (1976). Debt and disaster suddenly dominated the public view of Africa.

A radically changed international and domestic world brings us to the brink of a third post-war era, when the emerging image of Africa is one of marginality, if not total collapse. As scholarship re-orients to the domestic and international agendas we need to re-examine the intellectual and social legacies of the past two eras, and to apply experience and imagination to the redeployment of the very great assets they leave us with: from the tangible wealth of extraordinary libraries to the no-less valuable reservoirs of collegial networks and long-term theoretical orientations. These need to be reshaped and reconfigured, not intransigently defended or recklessly abandoned. An informed assessment of what these assets are and how they should be redeployed should start from people in the field itself, in the form of a self-study. The passages of this report that are written in the first person represent my own partisan contributions towards what should ultimately be a collective effort.

Chapter 1 presents my own view of how we are positioned on this new watershed, and Chapter 5 is a reconnaissance of three key issues that have already arisen in our debates: a) the contest and accommodation between area studies, international studies, and the disciplines; b) the social composition of our community and the intellectual influences this brings to bear; and c) the emerging assessments of our core intellectual commitments. These two Chapters can be read separately, along with the conclusions to the descriptive Chapters, as an interpretive essay. My suggestions about ways forward are contained in the conclusions to the descriptive Chapters, which have been regrouped, with an introduction, as Chapter 6.

Chapters 2, 3, and 4 are an attempt to be as comprehensive as possible about substantive components of African studies within the time frame for research. Since its foundation as a formally organized component of American academia almost fifty years ago African Studies has become an extraordinarily broad enterprise. Africa courses are taught at hundreds of universities and colleges; dozens offer certificates, minors and degrees; untold numbers of graduates work in NGOs, USAID and other development agencies. And each educational institution has its own particularities. I discovered, for example, that some of the most highly regarded semester abroad programs in Africa are run from colleges (St. Lawrence University and Kalamazoo College); the Berkeley program benefits from an endowment; Ohio State University has educated 250 Ugandans since 1965 under AID programs that have been budgeted at 16 million dollars (primarily for agricultural and economic research); innovative ecological and economic anthropological research has been fostered at SUNY-Binghamton under an AID cooperative agreement; Jack Parson in Charleston, South Carolina, and colleagues at Howard University have run a model OAU for undergraduates from between thirty and forty schools, annually for the past thirteen years; and only four universities (Iowa, Howard, Indiana and Northwestern) graduate as many as one third of their Africanist PhDs in the humanities. It no longer surprises me that the authors of the Hamilton-Hodges Report of 1987 concluded that the field was "fragmented.... None of the individuals interviewed had (or even claimed to have) a broad working knowledge of the field as a whole" and "almost without exception wanted to know what other institutions were doing" (1987:3). This kind of "fragmentation" represents an American success story, much as Lambert wrote about International Studies: "characteristically profuse, multicentric, and immensely inventive" (1986:2).

In presenting this complexity, as well as my own "take" on it, the image that I think best evokes its basic qualities is that of a micro-ecology.

The study of Africa is a small and very modestly funded component of academic life in this country, but it has flourished successfully in the terrain between the disciplines. It was founded and sustained in the beginning by foundations and government, which were concerned with the failure of the disciplines in American universities to promote international study. The parameters of area studies were defined by scholars who were based in the disciplines but worked on their borders, both theoretically and empirically. African Studies has been intermittently nourished, challenged and reshaped by infusions from new quarters and the interests of new participants: the development agencies in the 1970s and 1980s, and African-American constituencies and a stronger African presence by the early 1980s.

Like any micro-ecology, the study of Africa looks from time to time as if it could be washed away and reabsorbed into its component disciplines (or now into International Studies). But in the longer run that scenario turns out to have been the product of a passing phase or a particular vantage point. For example, an employment crisis was envisaged in African history as early as 1972 and PhD production started to stabilize, whereas interest in Africa continued to rise in other disciplines. An analysis of the Foreign Language and Area Studies Awards (FLAS) for the mid-1980s suggested that "political science might be approaching 'endangered species' status" (CIE 1995:5), whereas only a few years later government funding for study of the democratization movements has breathed new life into it. When crises have passed by, the endeavor is still there albeit often suffering painful losses and gaining new topics.

Survival has largely been due to the enduring originality of Africa, the intellectual power and commitment of the practitioners of African Studies, persisting links into the disciplines and funding agencies, and the adaptability that multiplicity ensures. Hence my effort to represent both a broad interpretation of "where we are" and some indication of old and new innovations. The ultimate focus is on the innovations that will have a disproportionate effect on the future, most importantly through the effect on recruitment of talent amongst the students and junior faculty. We, the current cohort of senior faculty, were educated in the basic research era, competed for careers and critiqued our disciplines during the development era, but are educating students and leading institutions under quite different conditions when the ecology has become much more intensely competitive. Competition produces excellence only up to a point; beyond that point, the hurdles become too high and the rewards too insecure for talented people to take the inevitable career risks. The question then is: what strategic resources at what key points can have a multiplier effect on the quality of work and the spirit of engagement amongst the African Studies community, and particularly its more

3

junior cohorts? The summaries of Chapters 2 through 4, presented in Chapter 6, offer some first suggestions that come out of the analyses of the rest of the report.

The reader is reminded that I am an economic anthropologist. Given the challenge of reviewing such a broad topic I have implicit recourse to my own discipline. I write from the assumption that resources are a basic component of any explanation, even where they do not explain everything. My division of our history into phases according to resource criteria and their corresponding orientations is clearly both partial and overdrawn. But it helps to develop a coherent framework for addressing the great complexity of this transitional moment.

1
THREE ORIENTATIONS IN THE SCHOLARSHIP ON AFRICA IN THE UNITED STATES

Two Past Eras and their Configurations: African Studies and the Study of Africa

There have been two great waves of interest in and training for Africa in U.S. academia: the great expansion of the 1960s in connection with Independence and the dynamics of the Cold War; and in the late 1970s and 1980s in connection with the vast infrastructural challenges of development in the context of highly-publicized drought, population growth, growing international debt and poverty. The first wave was focused on what its participants and funders saw as basic research: about culture and society, state building, and modernization. The second wave was devoted to a much greater degree to pressing and immediate problems of development. This change brought a quite marked branching of effort in the higher education devoted to Africa, between a) the African Studies created under the rubric of post-Independence Area Studies, oriented around in-depth field research, language study, history, anthropology and political science, and b) what I will refer to as the Study of Africa, utilizing survey methods and official databases, and comprising larger numbers of trainees in technical disciplines such as agricultural economics, education, and health.

When I argue that these represent two different configurations, I mean that each developed an internal logic to its conditions of existence: the basic concern that set the agenda determined the institutions involved and explains the sources of funding; the content of the training fit into the provisions of the funding (short term/long term; with/without specific requirements); and these allowed and promoted certain topics of research and kinds of scholarship. As it developed, each configuration also generated unforeseen, and not necessarily explicitly desired, consequences.

The forces that put in place the "canon" in African Studies were scientific concerns (about the diversity of human societies and their dynamics of change) that came out of social theory, and colonial and immediate post-colonial concerns with modernization. These prior concerns were already in place before the Cold War set in. The Cold War probably shaped some area studies a lot more than others. For Africa, so few were the American specialists and so lacking in strategic importance was most of the continent at that time, that the scholars were able to have considerable influence on the research agendas. They did so from the vantage point of classic history and classic social theories of change, together with the evolutionary theory informing the famous Africanist work in paleontology and archeology, and basic studies in linguistics. The resources available attracted some major scholars, and the extraordinary freedom they had for research and teaching allowed them to produce remarkably detailed works. For them, the area studies context afforded an institutional space for cultivating methodologies based on in-depth field research and—since their central interests were dynamics over time—for the linking of the social sciences with history. The development exigencies that arose in the 1970s brought a new pragmatic agenda, that increasingly cut into the resources available for basic research.

The careers of the present senior faculty for the most part cover an era during which theoretically-driven and pragmatically-driven research co-existed uneasily within the academy. The identities and career paths of trainees in the two endeavors diverged. African students and Americans in applied disciplines concentrated in the Study of Africa, funded by development programs, and a significant proportion of both African and American graduates went into careers outside the university in NGOs, ministries, and large development agencies. Many African Studies scholars saw the policy agendas as pursuing explicitly Cold War goals of political clientage, which—in the Africa of that time—supported enough dictators to discredit the whole enterprise in their eyes. Mutual distancing set in. The theoretical frameworks in the basic research branch shifted into the critique of development, largely drawing on inspiration from French and Latin American scholars. Creative work became comparative and analytical to a degree that was unprecedented within the old area studies format, but the area programs continued and greatly contributed to a new internationalism that was pushed forward by social theory. Underdevelopment theory reinforced the intellectual hierarchy between basic research in the academy, which was now international, theoretical and critical, and policy research, which tended to draw on Western-based models of change. Development institutes and applied departments expanded to meet the demand.

Networks and even the intellectual agendas, however, have never been entirely separate. But where they co-existed there was often tension as well as collaboration. The Study of Africa benefitted from the pre-existing resources of African Studies to a considerable degree, above all where both enterprises existed at the same university. Individual scholars continued to engage, especially when their theoretical work was about key issues of development such as agricultural growth, population and urbanization. Study of the "informal economy" was one important intellectual meeting place. In a very few places technical developmental studies, using survey research, quantification and model-building, came to be considered a pivotal component of theoretically-oriented area studies programs (Boston University in the 1980s; MSU in some disciplines; part of SUNY-Binghamton's work under a Cooperative Agreement with AID; a segment of the University of Wisconsin-Madison linked to the Land Tenure Center).

Mutual proximity revealed more starkly a different set of asymmetries than the intellectual ones between theoretical and applied work. Those of us who worked in universities where both endeavors existed saw the logics unfold. I was affiliated at Boston University African Studies Center from 1977 to 1994, and worked on issues in economic anthropology—such as agricultural change, household dynamics and urban food supply—that were part of the development agenda, so I witnessed both sides of what became a yawning gap in the resources available to ourselves and our development colleagues. While our colleagues in development were travelling back and forth to Africa for regular visits, the rest of us were finding it increasingly difficult and competitive to fund a research trip. For a summer in the field costing $10,000 *in toto* (including indirect costs) we submitted proposals to NSF, of 15 single-spaced pages plus a bibliography and supporting documents, at least nine months before the date of departure.

We were also finding it increasingly difficult to get away from university service and the conditions of career advancement. The rise of development studies coincided with other shifts within academia. Theoretical critique became the vehicle of intense competition for faculty positions and the orientations of departments. Administrations tested the waters for waves of the future with respect to student recruitment and external funds. This increasing attention to theory was driven by disciplinary forces rather than area studies, largely due to the fact that area studies do not control faculty positions in any but a very few universities. The forces that were unleashed affected everyone. Most influential was intensification of pressure to publish: for appointment, promotion and tenure purposes. In one sense, the return to the library did allow us to concentrate on the big picture, the long term and the essential conceptual and analytical issues. The SSRC overview papers published in the *African Studies Review* from 1981 to 1993 represent a high point of this era of "review and reconsideration" in African Studies. But there was a downside. The unforeseen result of the divergence for African Studies was the decreasing regular involvement of the theoretical wing in day-to-day Africa, and a certain myopia about the current state of Africa on the part of some in the academy. Much individual ingenuity went into keeping in touch. For example, many of us volunteered for the review boards of NGOs such as Oxfam-America. Some decided that taking advantage of the development resources was the only way to further their theoretical interests, but these tended to be scholars who could afford to be less ambitious for their academic careers, namely the established senior faculty who were not at risk, and various others who by personal situation or predilection opted for that route, complete with its irregularity of employment.

As a result, by the mid-to-late 1980s there developed a rising tide of frustration with us all on the part of Africa-based scholars, such as Mahmood Mamdani and Thandika Mkandawire, who saw our work as increasingly unrelated to African concerns, either intellectual or developmental. Even this very week there is a new publication arguing that we "use" Africa for career advancement rather than serve Africa's interests (Owomoyela 1994); "With friends like these...," his article is entitled. As I noted, this was not desired by anyone. In fact the founder of the canon in African history, Jan Vansina, has weighed in just as heavily about rushed and superficial research by comparison with the early years of the basic research orientation. But it is eminently understandable when viewed from the inside. The conditions of life shifted, and so did the extent and depth of field research in Africa that informed the scholarship. We developed two different endeavors, one prestigious and the other rich; the logics were simply working themselves out.

The work of that second era also became internally contentious for more encouraging reasons to do with growth. The humanities were late-starters in all this. There needed to be a critical mass of African literature and philosophy to come into routine publication for a substantial group of scholars to come into the academy. And there had to be a conceptual shift. Most of these domains of enquiry—music, knowledge, religion, oral poetics and art—had been folded into anthropology or ethno-hyphen studies (ethnomusicology, ethnophilosophy). During this second wave of research and training, the humanities started to struggle within African Studies to liberate themselves from the ethno-hyphen syndrome. And in creating intellectual space they have remained a source of important critical commentary on the other disciplines even though they are numerically much smaller. As intrinsically text-based, they also suffered far less than the social sciences from the limitations on funds and benefitted far more from the theoretical turn in the universities towards cultural studies. Luminaries in the African humanities can function—and have functioned—without regular travel to Africa.

At the same time the financial and political struggles associated with the winds of political change in Africa since structural adjustment (around 1985) brought an unprecedented number of fully trained and established African academic scholars (including very notably, francophone scholars) to

AFRICAN STUDIES IN THE UNITED STATES

jobs in the U.S. The middle-class and professional crisis in many parts of Africa greatly strengthened an African presence in international organizations and NGOs (largely in the social sciences and technical fields) and in academia (largely in the humanities). Francophone scholarship has two key characteristics that infuse the academic wing of African Studies with new inspiration (in addition to the brilliance of its particular exponents). It is indisputably "African," which links us back to the continent, or at the very least, to formerly unconsidered parts of African intellectual life. And it is "French" and philosophically oriented, which qualifies it squarely for the theoretical wing and thereby for representation in high-prestige research universities. The presence of a new cohort of senior African scholars in many of the institutions of African Studies (university departments, national committees and so on) very noticeably raised the profile of African intellectuals.

The resulting revitalization, especially in the African humanities, converged with a renewed African-American interest in African cultural dynamics and with the rising profile of African cultural production in the global media (even if some of it is produced in Pakistan and India).

The semi-independence of these two major branches of work during the 1980s, and their internal debates, account for the large number and complex nature of the whirlpools of debate as we move into another era. The image that is now projected of "African Studies" often reflects an over-stereotyped vision of one or the other branch, depending on the commentator's standpoint. For example, there is the odd coincidence that almost all reports on African Studies (including the last Ford Foundation Report) bemoan the low profile of economics while the statistics on dissertation production on Africa for that period show economics to be second only to education. The "economics" that is considered in short supply is actually that subsection of the discipline that is considered to fall within basic research, that is, to carry prestige. The bulk of Africanist dissertations in economics are in applied branches, and thereby "count" differently. The "prestige" wing of African Studies has also been far more productive of usable insights into development processes than is generally acknowledged by either side. For example, our critiques in the early 1980s of the standard assumption in economics of the household as a unitary decision-maker have now resulted in experiments with modelling the collective household, using game theory, and ultimately the claim of Paul Collier (1994) that a more sophisticated household economics is a direct contribution of African Studies to economics as a discipline. The same could be said of field-based research on the informal economy: "the real economy," as Janet MacGaffey called it.

At a moment of major change, therefore, there are dangers in continuing to frame the issues in terms of the limited vantage points provided by old stereotypes. Everything is liable to shift: the forces at work, the way they intersect, and all the varied interests that are brought along and reshaped. In addition to the danger of working with an irrelevant older stereotype there is the danger of developing a completely misleading new one. The urgency of a new view needs to be deeply tempered by the knowledge that there is now a much larger and more varied enterprise in African Studies that is only partially represented by any particular "view" at all. Debates on the brink of a third era need to be considered carefully, and not immediately interpreted as reflective of one or another polarization, or even as a confused maelstrom of differing perspectives. They are rather a frank tabling of important issues amongst the relevant—and remarkably committed—constituencies. In the present situation friction is to be expected. Resource scarcity and the image of an unpredictable future add an emotive edge to differing views of the road ahead that masks considerable funds of collaborative generosity. With that in mind, I suggest the outlines of the forces at work at present.

A New Era

The future of African Studies in American universities will result from the interplay of three very powerful forces: the situation in Africa, the reconfiguration of social investment throughout U.S. society, and the policies that universities adopt to resituate themselves for a new era of higher education. These forces are going to produce incoherencies and cross-purposes until they shake down into a pattern. No one's view of the future for African Studies is rosy, although for the present moment we enjoy a brief breather during which we should be regrouping.

One discovery of my research for this report has been the degree to which polarization is now a misleading image. As the world changed and the intellectual and political challenges intensified, the erudition and originality in the academic wing has been called upon to provide overviews, new directions of thinking and comparative observations. At the same time, the challenges have been on-the-ground, demanding detailed practical and procedural knowledge. Thus, since the late 1980s structural adjustment and democratization have recharged the "development" batteries and brought some

AFRICAN STUDIES IN THE UNITED STATES

African Studies scholars back into the policy debate, and back to residence and activism in Africa. In particular, of course, the revolutionary changes in South Africa that set in with Mandela's release exactly five years ago revitalized the scholar-development links. The detailed local knowledge afforded by field research and the long contemplation of its meaning, suddenly proved indispensable as all the political ground rules started changing at once. And the study of development agendas became a new frontier for academic analysis as we turned more and more towards understanding both sides of the interface between Africa and the West (see the Joint Committee on African Studies of the SSRC project of workshops and publications on development). Renewal of collaboration itself has brought us up sharply against the great need for new thinking.

Within the field, then, there are new collaborators in the engagement with change, and several different efforts to rethink the immediate past. We are all aware that approaches to the events in Somalia and the tragedy of Rwanda, let alone the forms of "globalization" into which any interpretation of them should fit, trail far behind the frontiers of actuality. Our students have been particularly bold in moving into new areas. They are studying AIDS, refugees and informal economies. The sense of the urgency of the African situation also brings constituencies together in new ways, or perhaps more accurately, throws a new spotlight on the value of old collaborations. Some specific controversies to the contrary—over the so-called "ghettoization" of African history (Curtin 1995) and certain well-known confrontations within the field (for a discussion of which see Chapter 5)—it should be widely recognized among white scholars that our African-American colleagues have been extraordinarily devoted to the sheer work of keeping the collective boat afloat, as well as trying to shift its direction.

Another important characteristic of the hiatus of the past four or five years is the turnover in leadership. Several of the directors of African Studies Centers are now African or African-American (Keller at UCLA, Bond at Columbia, Mowoe at Ohio State, and others at non-Title VI centers); several are women (Barnes at the University of Pennsylvania, Mann at Emory, myself at Northwestern); most are in their forties and early fifties; some Africanists who remain well-linked to us have moved into directorships of International Studies (Cohen at the University of Michigan, Robinson at Tufts, Watts at Berkeley, O'Meara at Indiana). Many of us are interlinked with one another through old collegial networks that we have yet to put to institutional service, and come from personal experiences and disciplinary histories that we have yet to bring fully to bear on the field as a whole. The key problem is that the efforts to rethink during this period of some rapprochement and momentary level-funding coincide with new uncertainties.

Uncertainties in Africa

The state of Africa, and US links to the continent—including the relations amongst scholarly, activist and artistic communities on both sides of the Atlantic—are all on the brink of deterioration. There can be few other large regions of the world where the maintenance of communications and the infrastructure for research are so challenging. At the same time, U.S. leadership is cutting down our official presence, suggesting that the end of the Cold War greatly diminishes our national interest in the continent and that the events in Somalia prove our incapacity to act effectively within an acceptable range of human and financial loss. Nine USAID missions have been closed and embassies have reduced their staffs. Our official policy is beginning to take on the title of "selective engagement:" with countries, sectors, problems and potential partners. Nigeria is the most discouraging of all cases. It comprises one fourth of the African population, and even greater proportions of its material wealth and trained intelligentsia. Since the reimposition of military rule, the country has become more dangerous to visit and our official presence has been greatly diminished by de-certification for financial interventions (due to the drug trade), and withdrawal of AID projects that feed into the official civil service.

The potential negative influence of this on the whole range of scholarship in and about Africa is very substantial, including—not least—the conditions of sheer physical safety of students doing study abroad or dissertation research. In my own view, we have yet to face the multiple direct and indirect effects of Somalia and Rwanda on the research enterprise. A recent article by an African-American journalist in the Washington Post, describing an "ancestral homeland where he never felt at home" (Richburg 1995:17), makes the effort to interest African-American students seem yet more difficult than the rest of us have faced. Maybe we will see increased avoidance, or maybe we will see renewed determination to understand and to carry out effective research. After all, this kind of political dynamic is by no means limited to Africa, and students can prove themselves to be remarkably bold. At a recent meeting about Fulbright applications, it was noted that the American student nominees have requested to go to 27 countries, while the senior researchers have requested to go to only 17. Even so, certain areas are being avoided: fully 40% of the applications are for the Southern Africa that Richburg found so much more congenial, and hardly anyone requests to visit Central Africa. Students and scholars are doing their own version of "selective engagement." The future of linkages is the only way to address this issue (see Chapter 2).

Uncertainties in Funding

The future of government funding for academic research and training has been saved from recision for this year only. What will happen in 1996 is unpredictable. African Studies has benefitted from foundation funding and NDEA grants to students through the early 1970s; Title VI funding for National Resource Centers since the mid-1960s; large AID-funded research projects and AID/ATLAS training for African students since the early 1970s; foundation funding for SSRC and particular projects; the Fulbright program; the usual disciplinary funding through NSF, NEH, NEA, NIH and so on; and, indirectly but importantly, the Peace Corps, throughout the past thirty years. Most of these programs are potentially vulnerable to federal budget cuts.

No one can yet predict the volume or the programmatic balance of the cuts that will certainly come next year. Several entire agencies which support African Studies are threatened with elimination or assimilation to other units of government in an attempt to "clear the decks:" the Department of Education, USAID, and NEH. Cuts are expected in all the others. Since I take up the funding issues in Chapter 3, with respect to training, and Chapter 4, with respect to programs, suffice it here to say that government funding is liable to continue but on a reduced and redirected basis.

Uncertainties in the Universities

The commitment of universities to these domains of enquiry is very much on the table for consideration, even though—as I will show in Chapter 4—we have been spared the first round of reorganizations and budget cuts. We are moving into an era in which standards of "productivity" are being reassessed for higher education. These will include numbers of students, speed of degree-completion, and the generation of outside funding as well as the university's reputation for "excellence" and thereby its comparative prestige. The latter sounds vague but it is a very real element in the calculation because

13

universities have differential access to research grants and endowment funds according to their prestige and the excellence of the scholarship they enable. Particular universities have reputations in particular areas, and particular scholars can enormously raise the profile and "productivity" of even quite small fields.

Administrators will be asking what African Studies programs contribute to one or other of the measures of productivity. Programs at different universities will have different "strong suits" in this regard, and are therefore likely to diversify much further than they have already (and the generally-standardized Title VI began to reflect this in the last round of funding, although perhaps not strongly enough). My own sense is that the numbers/income/constituency criteria for productivity will start to part company with the theory/prestige criteria, not this time on the basis of the development/academic divergence, but around a differentiation of the "constituencies" between those who have an ethnic and general educational goal for studying the world outside the U.S., and those whose interests remain in theoretical critique of the fundamental suppositions of analytical categories for understanding the world at large, including the U.S. We are already witnessing differentiation of faculties on these grounds: to take the Duke example, into professors "of the practice of," and just "professors." But differentiation must surely echo pressures within the world of U.S. academia such that only some universities and some subjects will remain in the "research" tier. African Studies is like all area and international studies at the university, in that it can go in either direction: one that focuses on teaching a constituency, another that focuses on honing the intellectual toolkit.

Within the university this vast shift is setting up confusions and contradictions in the disciplines to which we belong. The first results from the disciplines that house the old core of African Studies. Since the quasi-totality of "African Studies" appointments are in disciplines (except at Howard University, where African Studies is a department), any pressures on the disciplines will have important effects on interdisciplinary studies. The Bowen and Rudenstine study of PhD training showed that departmental "productivity" (in years to completion and proportion of attrition) is much lower in our core disciplines than in the sciences, although the doctoral students are classically also teaching assistants for large numbers of undergraduates. Prestige in these disciplines rests on dissertations being, as one colleague put it, "paradigm-making," which takes much longer than the scientific apprenticeship followed by a postdoctoral fellowship. So the criteria of productivity are running counter to each other: producing excellence in our disciplines is labor-intensive for all concerned, and increasingly incompatible with a quantitative measure of cost effectiveness in the production of large constituencies of students and professionally trained graduates. As a result, we expect university investment in graduate training in all these disciplines to be under close scrutiny.

In the rearrangements, the retention of an Africanist component will vary by discipline according to Africa's past contribution to what is seen as the current "cutting edge." Stellar individual scholars aside, for example, Africa is more important to anthropology than to any other constituted discipline; it has a strong niche in history; probably a lower profile in the social science disciplines that depend on quantitative data (economics and political science) in part because of the nature of the sources; and a low but rising profile in the humanities. We argue strongly for intellectual originality in these contexts (see the recent book *Africa and the Disciplines*), and experience may well bear us out that current world dynamics demand study with field-based techniques as well as models. Engaging vigorously with our respective disciplines on these grounds is one major way that we will retain a place in theoretical scholarship and the research universities.

The other general force affecting us is the administrative thrust to promote teaching and scholarship in response to numbers of constituents. State universities in particular have to address the tax-payers, in all their multi-cultural forms. There is a rising profile to the demand by American ethnic constituencies and foreign nationals for formal study of "their" area of the world. In some cases ethnic communities have contributed to the funding of their area studies center, particularly at the public universities. But the demand is felt far more broadly, and is part of a shift towards more explicit accountability, often by quantitative criteria. Can these interests be folded into "International Studies" (as universities may want to do in the interests of costs) and still maintain ethnic allegiances? Are they stable enough as foundations for institution-building as government has been? (Probably not, hence the university concern with building endowments to replace government allocations of various sorts). Will the most powerful of them (Japanese, for example) prefer to invest in fields that have no area studies component at all (such as engineering)? Will they favor the arts, national heritage and cultural innovations that have a marketable potential? Most seriously for all classic conceptions of scholarship, has the relativity of knowledge that was promoted by post-modernism cleared the way for a kind of scholarship that no longer aims for critical thinking about empirical problems? How will we recognize this and reconcile the scientific and accountability agendas? What will universities—as larger intellectual communities comprising the sciences as well—do about it? No-one knows the answers to these questions, although I take up the beginnings of our own debates on them in Chapter 4.

Much, then, will depend on the state of the particular area, its ethnic constituency in the U.S., and the vision and response of scholars and other leaders who are in a position to nudge particular institutions in one direction or another at this moment of change. The small constituency for Africa could be a cloud with a silver lining in the short run. We have the benefit of a moment for contemplation and debate, before the pressures of a constituency-oriented agenda set in. African Studies benefits from several great strengths alongside its obvious problems. It is the main area of the world in which the fieldwork tradition and interdisciplinary study have been imperative and highly fruitful, which accounts for much of the intellectual originality that its scholars bring to their disciplines. The level of commitment by scholars has been extraordinarily high, and the social composition of both the theoretical and the applied branches is now more diverse than it has been, and at the senior level. Very sound infrastructures exist (libraries, cost-sharing by universities, programs, intellectual and physical space, high quality faculties), which have been used to leverage a variety of further support and a vast range of activities, considering the size of the budgets.

In my own view combining the past assets and current challenges creates an intellectual potential that has never looked brighter, in spite of the imminent threats to research and training funds. We are moving ahead on the basis of thematic and collaborative research: on environmental issues, population, the principles underlying endogenous knowledge, the place of Africa in world labor history, the history of African wealth, and other topics. The watershed moment is fostering different kinds of interdisciplinary effort than the history-anthropology mutual influence of the past. Both disciplines have gone beyond the frontier stage in their mutual collaboration, which opens up great potential for new kinds of comparative and analytical agendas with other disciplines as well. The combined uncertainties, however, as we move unsteadily towards the constituency-oriented work that has set in more forcefully elsewhere in the academy, creates a situation of such tension and enervating demands from all sides that it is difficult to organize around strategic ways forward.

As the debates produce both heat and light in unpredictable ways, the particular challenge to be kept in focus is to redefine the terms under which the past competitiveness of Africa in attracting young scholars and generating new work within the American academy can be reshaped and carried forward. American academic life is very competitive at every stage, and becoming more

16

so. All logics of profound discouragement to the contrary, there is presently no dearth of strong candidates for taking on scholarship about Africa. This makes the content of training we offer them critically important. Many of us think that we may no longer be nurturing and developing students along lines that are adequate to the situation of research and the job market. Thematic research in new disciplinary configurations implies new kinds of training, whose results in turn can help us to make use of the thematic "interlude" as a contribution to the future of African Studies institutions and not only its accumulated base of knowledge.

Ideally this survey should be a collective enterprise. A start has already been made: the book *Africa and the Disciplines*, published in 1994; overviews by African scholars of the intellectual situation in Africa (Mkandawire 1993), of the scholarship in North American journals (Zeleza) and the political context of all our work (Chege 1994); a conference on "Reconstructing the Study and Meaning of Africa" at Urbana in 1994; a 1995 special number of *ISSUE* (23/1) devoted to the future of African Studies; and another conference, on "Scholarly Authority," at Northwestern in April of 1995. The issues of intellectual focus that are shaped by the social composition of the community of scholars necessarily come first; witness the title of the opening address to the Urbana conference "The Decline of the Africanists' Africa and the Rise of new Africas." But the situation is yet more convoluted and demanding than this, and a whole set of questions—whose resolution will shape the next configuration of African Studies—awaits in the wings.

2
LINKAGES WITH AFRICA

The networks of connection with Africa are the foundation of African Studies. However much armchair thought goes on, or analysis of data sets, it is travel to Africa that recruits and commits students, fieldwork in Africa that generates the best work, frequent exchanges with African colleagues that creates intellectual communities, and constant contact that reconfirms the sense of relevance without which the work would lack inspiration. Opportunities to "be there" and to bring Africans here also helps to create a constituency for Africa in this country.

Africa is unique in the American ethnic world in that, until the most recent wave of immigrants, its American descendants have been unable to retain and recreate the multitude of personal connections that links other ethnic populations to their places of origin. Private travel, and probably even communication, is much lower than the size of the population could support. This is a major impoverishment, and means that linkage programs have to be organized and funded, even when their greatest benefit is largely the kind of exposure that would normally arise from visiting the family, taking a vacation or pursuing a passionate hobby. Americans go to Africa for specific reasons. The reasons that directly affect academic African Studies are a) the general exposure that brings in committed students, b) research opportunities, c) exchanges that enliven and strengthen university communities, and d) scholarly networks for specific collective scientific goals. Because it is so expensive in time and money, and has to make up for so much, the creation of effective linkages with Africa depends on careful assessment of what it is they are trying to achieve.

The possibility of linkage has waxed and waned over the history of African Studies, and so have the models for creating it. Because of the heterogeneity and sudden changes it has been difficult for me to be systematic about this topic. Aili Mari Tripp did a useful review of international exchanges in 1991, and shows how suddenly and drastically the numbers of exchanges to Africa that were financed under U.S. Government International Academic Exchanges fell between 1986 and 1990 alone: from 535 to 206. The numbers of students funded through federal international exchange programs have fallen disproportionately to others; according to the J. William Fulbright Scholarship Board, student awards have decreased by 50% since 1953, while faculty awards increased over the same period by close to 70%. She writes "The overwhelming majority of U.S. students abroad study in Europe (75%), while only 9.2% study in Latin America....and 1.2% in Africa" (1991:75).

AFRICAN STUDIES IN THE UNITED STATES

It is not easy to counter such massive shifts. The sheer numbers, the experience of programs folding when African governments have changed or the universities went on strike, create the impression that the whole enterprise is for all practical purposes in receivership. I doubt that this is the case, although the combined effect of the medical risks, insecurity, the rising cost of air travel to the continent and the appalling state of communications all make it a very great challenge. Last year (1994) was a particularly dreadful year for creating the kind of positive image of Africa that would invite Americans to devote resources to building linkages. The *Hot Zone*, Kaplan's article on "The Coming Anarchy," the coverage of the Rwanda genocide, and the T.V. special on corruption in Nigeria would surely sow panic about Africa into the hearts of protective American parents and safety-conscious American professionals. Famous and wealthy advocates for Africa have never been there, never learned to greet in an African language.

On the other side of the ocean, the sudden collapse of professional salaries in Africa that resulted from devaluation in the mid-1980s, makes foreign travel, the library phase of writing and research, and the learning of new techniques impossible for African colleagues. Civil war and political domination add their own effects. A spiral has been set up: limited libraries means limited linkage of African scholarship to disciplinary literature, which in turn reduces the possibility of publication and thereby reinforces the centrality of western scholarship and the potential for mutual insularity. Some people have worked extremely hard to avoid the obvious downward logic, but the fate of the universities in Africa remains a source of visible grief to our African colleagues.

I think, on the other hand, that members of the American university community have become much more mobile in recent years, and visit a great many places *for relatively short periods of time*, between a couple of weeks and six months. Certain specific places in Africa may well attract this kind of visitor. For example, a group of thirty Northwestern business school students have just organized and self-financed a three week visit to South Africa. Last year a comparable group went to Ghana. I heard that an African-American sorority sponsors an Africa visit for students. Several of our applicants to the graduate program this year have been to Africa more than once as undergraduates: to study, work and do research. One—an African-American—studied prisoners! Even anthropological research is beginning to be done in multiple shorter stints, rather than the two year total immersion of the Malinowski model. Forty six universities applied to USIA this year for activities in Africa under its Affiliations program. Every Title VI center has

20

AFRICAN STUDIES IN THE UNITED STATES

several affiliations for various purposes. In other words, at least some subsection of the potential constituents for exchanges with Africa has not given up, even if it means mobilizing private funds. There must be a distinctive group that is energized by adversity rather than intimidated by it. A cohort of my own graduate students carried out their research with great success under desperately difficult personal conditions that must vie with anything taken on by earlier generations of researchers.

The slow-but-sure development of e-mail and the Internet will greatly improve communications. There are already people in the health field who are working on the potentials of distance learning modules as well as general networking of ideas, plans, research results, drafts of papers and so on. The possibilities are very wide and a lot of experimentation will go on in the near future. A colleague with much experience in USAID claims that her African support staff have always shown extraordinary facility with computer learning, with mid-levels of formal education. In theory then, electronic communications could eventually be the complete answer to the book drought and the lack of access to journals. It's a long road, however, requiring reliable electrical and phone systems, up-to-date computers, and so on.

There are dangers in fostering short visits. They can never make up for the long immersion that has produced the seminal work of the past, but they do seem to be a workable solution to the multiple challenges, none of which is going away. The question then is: what optimal forms can shorter-term visits take, for students and scholars from both sides of the Atlantic? How can some long-term immersion be preserved for Americans, and some long-term library and training update opportunities for Africans?

All three professional levels are important. According to the responses to my request for information from college and university programs, early and intense exposure seems to be the single most important factor in creating the kind of life-long commitment that animates later scholarly creativity. The Peace Corps and other NGO service probably constitute the greatest contribution to general knowledge about, and commitment to, Africa in the U.S. population. (I tried to generate figures on numbers of volunteers, by country, but apparently the data are not compiled in that way.) Peace Corps returnees constitute a significant proportion of the academic African Studies community. Non-academic returnees are highly represented among the supporters of NGOs and of all activities around their area.

If there is a single point at which long immersion should be preserved at all costs it is at the dissertation stage. This period is not only intellectually formative and productive of the essential professional qualification; it sets in place the assets of knowledge, language and collegial networks that last a professional lifetime. These, in turn, make possible fruitful shorter visits at later stages. It can hardly be stated forcefully enough to those outside our field that *all* the seminal work has been done by scholars who have been forced by long stay and consistent exposure to take on the originality of Africa in a profound and analytically critical way. Only in certain limited disciplines, such as literature, is this possible without fieldwork. Senior scholars have the relative flexibility and resources to figure out for themselves how to incorporate the need to do long-term field research. At that level the most pressing needs in the area of exchange are visits that maintain and extend networks so that important research topics can be defined and addressed collaboratively, and so that African colleagues are able to get a period of peace and quiet so that they can think, study and write.

I am very hopeful about one kind of initiative for each level: a) opportunities for undergraduates that involve an element of work, whether that be research or service (as distinct from the classic "semester abroad" model); b) the maintenance of the fieldwork basis of dissertation study in its present form (although better supported by prior methodological training and experience, as discussed in the following Chapter); and c) faculty collaborations for defined purposes, if possible allowing three-way linkages between institutions or the activation of wider networks (as distinct from the classic two-party, generalized long term commitment).

Before giving examples I should provide a sense of the kind of exchange already in place at each level.

Undergraduates

Several universities have regular summer or semester abroad programs that have good track records: the Boston University program in Niger, Iowa and University of Pennsylvania in Nigeria, Wisconsin in Senegal, and Kalamazoo College and St. Lawrence in Kenya, *et al.* Each attracts students from other schools. I believe that there is a rapid move to create such programs in South Africa. The class preparation of students for the trip seems varied, according to anecdotal evidence, and a study of the St. Lawrence alumni suggested that they needed a capstone course when they returned to campus to fit together what remained for many "fractured images."

My most complete source is on the St. Lawrence program, which takes two groups of up to 30 students a year to Kenya, and provides 2 full scholarships a year for Kenyan students to attend the university. Two particular professors have worked on the program continuously for thirteen years, which must undoubtedly account for its continuing refinement.

In the interests of brevity I want to draw three points out of their self-study. First, by far the largest group to go on the program became interested in African Studies through another student, far more than through a course, instructor or prior interest. Personal networks, through which the intangible quality of passionate enthusiasm is conveyed, still play a decisive role. Undergraduate projects have to be explicitly geared towards creating such networks, above all for students who might not automatically be linked into them, such as students at HBCUs. Students are clearly not motivated to take action by identity alone; neither can they easily facilitate their own links. While the content of programs needs to be substantial, their capacity to create relationships for the undergraduates is a goal that should not be occluded.

Secondly, many of the students come from particular disciplines. In a letter the coordinator, Celia Nyamweru, suggested that environmental studies and anthropology/sociology seem to be most important in their own program. Ideally, then, one would match student interest with targeted work. Certainly one or two programs I know of do specialize; for example, there is one that studies dance in Senegal, and another from Rhode Island School of Design that studies weaving in West Africa. Possibly there are obvious and important topics that are not covered, that could be beneficial to both African and American students, where the class and work standards were pitched at a high level. I don't know, for example, whether there are programs in music, performative arts, film/media or pre-med. What about, for example, a visit to Ghana for performance majors that involved working on arrangements for Panafest and culminated in attending the festival? Or a visit to Ouagadougou about film, that culminated in being at the film festival? Or pre-med programs in health projects? I would also think that some topics would attract more African-American interest than others, to get around the problem that the general "study abroad" package, with home stay etc., has been more attractive to (and affordable by) the classic liberal arts major from a white middle class background. A specialist experience adds to work skills and future professional networks.

Thirdly, whether matched or not, "Many alumni felt that the most important learning experiences offered by the program can only be found when students venture out on their own...[for] internships...." Again, the work/living experience seems to make a difference. In the Boston University Niger project, the internship component makes a big impression.

AFRICAN STUDIES IN THE UNITED STATES

Clearly undergraduate study/work abroad pays off many times over because it feeds information and enthusiasm into the vast networks of youth. By comparison, the graduate and professional networks are quite narrow. There is a fairly vast fund of experience in these programs, which I have hardly tapped here; compiling the views of several experts about their "dream" exchange program would create a very worthwhile resource.

Dissertation work

A lot of planning has already gone into improving conditions for research, including pre-dissertation visits financed through the Social Science Research Council and the persisting encouragement of the interdisciplinary African Studies faculty to plan to undertake research trips of a year or more. We have to keep reiterating the same message, and supporting it.

Faculty exchange

I have suggested that one of the real and disastrous casualties of the past era has been the declining presence of Africa as a regular reality in the lives of many American faculty. The old model of teaching in an African university is no longer possible, except perhaps in Southern Africa. Berkeley, for example, is developing coursework with the University of Durban-Westview, and Michigan State has had a project with the University of Zimbabwe which has produced 190 collaborative publications, 300 faculty and student exchanges, and undergraduate study-abroad. Ohio State collaborates with the College of Agriculture in Swaziland.

Other institutional exchanges are mainly for short courses: Ohio State has a link for 6-week courses with the College of Law and the Institute of Advanced Legal Studies of the University of Lagos. As I will mention later, the revisions of the USIA programs in Africa propose to strengthen institutional exchanges. The commentaries make it clear that most faculty feel that this kind of link is neither adequate nor in line with current realities in the universities. Relations can be cumbersome, expensive and frustrating.

The growing forms of organization for scholars in Africa are the network and the association. Several are formalized: CODESRIA (Council for the Development of Economic and Social Research in Africa), based in Dakar, is the largest, with about 800 individual members; there is a relatively new Association of African Anthropologists; OSSREA (Organization for Social Science Research in East Africa) brings in scholars from Ethiopia to Tanzania, and perhaps further south; WARC (the West African Research Center) in Dakar is new, and largely devoted to the humanities.

On our own side, we have yet to develop comparable organizations to interface successfully. Our own professional groups are extremely large, and do not manage funding, research and study to the same degree that the African organizations do. We search for rubrics under which to connect: the important topic for debate that could generate a joint conference; the fellowship program that could bring a small group with related interests together for a period of joint residence, after the model of the Institutes for Advanced Study in Palo Alto and Princeton, or to match individuals with resources, after the model of the Bunting Institute at Radcliffe. Our own resources are localized, even though our connections with one another are far-flung.

I have co-organized and struggled to fund several conferences involving both African and American researchers: two in Africa, two in the U.S. and one coming up in Europe. It is very hard work. We do have to localize in order to benefit from existing assets. Under present conditions of budget cuts it is unlikely that new assets will be created. Spreading of the linkages may demand strategic work through particular nodes that are already in place, possibly along some thematic lines, so that collective intellectual pressure can be sustained on urgent topics. In many contexts we are already managing to achieve this, but by the sweat of everyone's brow and not to maximal advantage to bring in the younger African scholars.

Scholars in their thirties in Africa must be the most neglected group of all. Their immediate seniors have been able to get jobs elsewhere (including in South Africa) or can tap into international funding. Something as modest as extra funding for two or three junior scholars to attend meetings or spend 6 weeks abroad, through nodes of linkage that could hook them up to larger networks, could pay off very well. Again, there are examples: a Beninois sociologist who spent three months at Northwestern last fall, through a WARC fellowship; a Cameroonian B.Sc.-level botanist, who may be linked into an agriculture project. If we were better able to place people appropriately and in a timely manner, and to draw on the knowledge in the CODESRIA, OSSREA, WARC, etc. networks, the multiplier effects would be greater.

These challenges are particularly acute in the basic research disciplines. By comparison, relatively vast networks and opportunities have been afforded to students and faculty through the development wing, although my research for the report did not go so far as to explore their effectivity for junior scholars in career academic appointments.

3
PATTERNS OF ADVANCED TRAINING IN AFRICAN STUDIES

Numbers, Nationalities and Disciplines

"Reports of decline in research about Africa are not supported by the numbers of dissertations produced each year" (Lauer 1989:183).

The earliest concerns about the future of African Studies graduate training were expressed around 1972—almost a quarter century ago—when "[f]unding became scarcer, and it was clear that an employment crisis loomed on the horizon" (Vansina 1994:143). For at least twenty years such fears for the future have coexisted with increasing numbers of students in graduate training. In spite of all the apparent disincentives, by 1984 dissertations about Africa had not only risen sharply in absolute numbers, they had almost doubled since the 1960s in their share of total North American dissertations (from 0.82% in 1964 to 1.48% in 1984 [Lauer 1989:197]). Graduate study is long, expensive and risky. In African Studies it means learning languages that are difficult (for native speakers of European languages), spoken by relatively small populations, and that cannot be used elsewhere. It means engaging with a part of the world that has only ever been of peripheral strategic interest to the U.S., and taking increasingly serious health risks. In the 1980s and 1990s, to choose graduate training in African Studies has meant very smart people forgoing careers in rapidly expanding job markets in finance and computers, some of whom come into graduate school already equipped with computer skills that could earn them a good living. All evidence from faculty suggests that the quality of doctoral applicants is still high. At the end, the graduate faces an uncertain job market, in an academia that is shifting emphasis from graduate to undergraduate teaching, where the competition for positions, grants and tenure is fierce. Maturity does not seem to affect matters; both the statistics and people's impressions suggest that "graduate students in African Studies are relatively older than might be expected" (NCASA 1991:13). On the face of it, then, the demand for graduate training in African Studies is a mystery.

Joseph Lauer is the acknowledged compiler of records on higher education in African Studies. The crude numbers with respect to dissertation production on Africa in the USA, since 1951, are as follows:

AFRICAN STUDIES IN THE UNITED STATES

Table 1:
Average Annual Dissertation Production, 1951-93

Years	Annual Average Dissertation Production
1951-60	49
1961-65	105
1966-70	208
1972-78	245
1979-83	370
1984-86	440
1987-93	449

Sources: Lauer 1989; Lauer Notes Feb 7th 1995.
(Note: North Africa is included. Lauer suggests using these numbers with "caution," for a whole set of procedural reasons, but they provide invaluable guidelines.)

The disciplines, however, follow semi-independent patterns of growth and change, as might be expected, and training and research about Africa can change in composition without changing the total volume. Unlike the overall trend, dissertation production in African history peaked in the mid-1970s and then almost halved by the mid-1980s (NCASA 1991:13). In fact, this pattern of change in historical scholarship may well account for the general sense of decline to which many allude, since the same report notes in its comparative conclusions, "it is history that dominates area studies" (p 75) in numbers of faculty appointments. Anthropology, by contrast, may have held its own or even advanced a little: for 1980-86 Africa claimed 12% of applications to the NSF Anthropology Program (which includes Archeology and Biological Anthropology), with a success rate of 31%; in 1986-91 Africanists submitted 13% of proposals, and had the tied-highest success rate of 40% (Plattner, Hamilton and Madden 1987; Plattner and McIntyre 1991; Plattner, Aronson and Abellera 1993).

We tabulated dissertations by discipline, as reported in the *ASA News*, for the years 1986-94, to compare with the figures for 1974-87 produced by Lauer. His admonitions to caution apply; note, for example, that for the first period the 1987 numbers may have been incomplete, and for the second, the 1994 numbers were certainly incompletely submitted by the time the record was calculated. But the figures do provide strongly suggestive guidelines.

AFRICAN STUDIES IN THE UNITED STATES

Table 2:
Total Dissertation Production, by Discipline, 1974-87 and 1986-94

Discipline/Field	1974-87		1986-94	
	#	Rank Order	#	Rank Order
Agriculture	124	15	145	10
Anthropology	528	5	289	5
Arts	150	13	87	13
Communications	152	12	87	13
Economics and Business	796	2	402	2
Education	1,370	1	553	1
Geography	134	14	70	14
Health Sciences	168	11	no category	
History	638	4	255	6
Language	248	9	178	9
Law	no category		4	
Library Science	no category		14	
Literature	322	7	210	8
Natural and Applied Sciences	312	8	337	4
Philosophy, Religion and Theology	196	10	137	11
Political Science	794	3	373	3
Psychology	no category		8	
Sociology	372	6	225	7
Urban and Regional Planning	107	16	94	12

*Source: Lauer for 1974-87; ASA News, data reported by Lauer,
compiled by Kemp, for 1986-94.*

There are two striking inferences to be made here. First, economics, business and education—none of which is represented in the classic area studies format and most of which would be based in professional schools rather than colleges of arts and sciences—have been a far more important part of training relative to Africa than has normally been recognized, and they have held their own over time. Secondly, agriculture, the sciences, and planning have risen marginally in the rankings, with the more classic area studies disciplines (history, political science, anthropology and the humanities) maintaining or losing ground a notch or two. One plausible interpretation would be that policy-relevance has been a strong and strengthening criterion for dissertation research.

To some degree this pattern must reflect research funding. But it probably also reflects the national origins of graduate students. The US educates the world at the more advanced levels, including Africa. Using the very rough criterion of a recognizably African name as dissertation author, we looked at the disciplinary distribution of African versus non-African students. The results, for 1986-94, are as follows:

Table 3:
Percentage of African Dissertation Authors by Discipline, 1986-94

Discipline	% African Authors
Agriculture	74
Anthropology	18
Planning/Architecture	68
Communications	71
Economics, business	64
Education	74
Fine Arts	30
Geography	41
History	33
Law	100
Library Science	93
Languages and Linguistics	58
Literature and Folklore	47
Philosophy, Religion, Theology	47
Political Science	54
Psychology	75
Sciences/Engineering	47
Sociology	70
Total for all disciplines	55

Source: Data from ASA News. Reported by Lauer, compiled by Kemp.

Of course, some African students will be US citizens, so the inferences have to be carefully drawn. There is, however, a rather striking distribution here, with African students concentrated in what are understood in our own educational systems to be "applied fields," while the more theoretical disciplines are still over half non-African.

Different commentators would see very different dynamics here: one might deplore the lack of support for African scholarship in the disciplines that have high intellectual profiles while another might applaud the greater concentration of African work in disciplines that are considered to have greater relevance to the immediate challenges of the continent, and yet another might simply see a lag time between the two, since a rising proportion of scholars who originate from the "areas" of area studies seems to be a general pattern. For example, Raphael reports that "as of 1989, the majority—about two thirds—of Ph.D. dissertations written in this country with a Southeast Asian focus have been written by Southeast Asian scholars and...the most important works in the area will be written, if they aren't already, by those living there" (1994:99). By these comparative criteria, African Studies in the U.S. is a few percentage points behind Southeast Asia in its education of nationals and Americans who originate from the region. It may be that the policy-relevant disciplines represent the wedge into American higher education, and the intellectual breadth will follow. One version of this view, which I and many others share, is that policy relevance and intellectual profile should converge at some points. As the world changes, the nature of those changes becomes an intellectual agenda of the highest order. The mechanization of agriculture and the use of contraceptives are not simply technical decisions to be studied in applied disciplines, for instance, but part of the global system. And those who study the global system can no longer be illiterate with respect to the "technicalities" through which visions are turned into realities.

One of the forces behind the emphasis on applied disciplines during the 1980s must surely be the USAID effort to train Africans in the U.S. Many have been trained to the PhD level through the ATLAS/AFGRAD program run through the African American Institute. AFGRAD provided US academic training (at all levels) for over 3,000 Africans from 46 countries (ATLAS Brochure). The ATLAS project explicitly targets "disciplines critical to development such as economics, business administration, public health, agriculture and engineering"; there is a special focus on the education of women; and the institutional oversight involves both development and academic agencies (AID, AAI, the Council of Graduate Schools, The African Academy of Sciences, The National Association for Equal Opportunity Higher Education [which represents 117 HBCUs]), Arthur D. Little, Management Systems International, and the host countries).

31

AFRICAN STUDIES IN THE UNITED STATES

The ATLAS project has clearly been large enough to affect the African Studies student body and the distribution of dissertations. According to the faculty, the number of African students who are financed by their families or governments is very small and declining, in contrast to the financial support for students from other areas of the world. Changes in U.S. national policy will therefore have a very great effect on the profile of our student body in African Studies.

There seem to be two different enterprises here—the core area studies disciplines, that are still more than 50% American, and the applied disciplines that are often over 75% African. Do they both go on at the same academic institutions, benefitting from shared intellectual and library resources, collegiality and faculty expertise in the particular challenges of research in Africa? Again we used a rough measure to gauge the overlap: the proportion of PhD dissertations in each discipline that was produced between 1986 and 1994 by the federally-funded Title VI centers (taken as a group), and the proportion of those that were African-authored. This does not really allow us to infer directly the influence of Title VI status because most of the National Resource Centers in the area studies are at large public universities that have strong applied training programs (through Land Grant status, for example), lower tuition and often stellar reputations as well; hence, they would clearly attract some students regardless of the federal support. Obviously there is African research expertise at other universities as well, although the quality of the library resources may be very inferior. It is worth noting here that the major African Studies Programs are blessed with absolutely extraordinary librarians, who basically serve the needs of the entire research community.

With these provisos in mind, we can still get some sense of the theoretical/applied synergies by making a tabulation of the type of university from which degrees are being granted in "African Studies" and "The Study of Africa."

Table 4:

Percentage of Africanist Dissertations produced at Title VI Centers, and the Percentage of These that are African Authored

Discipline	% Africanist Dissertations Title VI	% of These African-Authored
Agriculture	26	62
Anthropology	28	24
Planning	23	64
Communications	49	76
Economics/Business	26	57
Education	30	69
Fine Arts	50	23
Geography	19	16
History	47	27
Linguistics/Language	50	52
Literature/Folklore	38	49
Philosophy/Religion/Theology	9	33
Political Science	26	40
Sciences/Engineering	18	44
Sociology	24	68

Source: ASA News. Data reported by Lauer, compiled by Kemp.
(Note: Small numbers for column 2 in Geography and Philosophy place these data outside of consideration.)

AFRICAN STUDIES IN THE UNITED STATES

The universities with Title VI centers produced 30% of all Africa-related PhD dissertations 1986-94, and 27% of all dissertations by scholars with African names. They were particularly predominant in History, Languages, Literature and the Arts, with all the social sciences grouping at about 25% of Africanist dissertations produced. The African scholars are distributed similarly in Title VI centers as in higher education in general: considerably more diffused in agriculture, philosophy/theology and political science; a little more diffused in economics/business and most other disciplines; more concentrated in anthropology and communications. In brief, then, Title VI supports some disciplines more than others, but seems to affect the location of African scholars in African Studies/The Study of Africa relatively little. African scholars are neither flooding into the Title VI centers nor avoiding them.

This pattern is somewhat mysterious, given the long-term federal investment in area studies centers. Criteria for student placement other than Africa expertise must be at work. Disciplinary strength is undoubtedly one of these, especially for health and demography, which are best represented in institutions other than the Title VI universities. Remote sensing is particularly strong at Maryland-College Park; International Relations may be stronger in the Washington, D.C.-area schools. The local agro-ecology of the region where the university is located may be important for agriculture training; further south may make more sense than Michigan for some students. And pressures to distribute federal resources more broadly than the "same old" places may well play a part as representatives in D.C. lobby for their own academic institutions.

How well this dispersion works to foster good research is debatable. Several years ago, out of concern for the preparation of agriculture students for research in Africa, The Rockefeller Foundation instituted special sessions of summer training for African doctoral students, held at the Land Tenure Center at the University of Wisconsin-Madison (a Title VI Center). Even so, they are still concerned about the adequacy of the training for research in an African context that is shown in the applications for their research grants for African students (the ADIA project, reviewed by Watts 1994). The element that seems lacking in the proposals submitted to their fellowship competition is rigorous and pragmatic training in field research techniques, as distinct from the standardized methods used for research in countries with reliable and complete official data sets and populations who can participate in phone and mail surveys. (It should be noted that the AFGRAD/ATLAS scholars would

34

not appear in the Rockefeller pool since their entire education is covered by the program, presumably to ensure that investment in their carefully selected candidates is not wasted by the inevitable attrition attendant on competition for research funds.)

One cannot leave this topic of a perceived differential quality of training between African Studies and The Study of Africa without mentioning the sensitive issue of recruitment. African Studies faculty across the board endorse the competitive process: for acceptance to graduate school, research funds, exams, jobs and so on. Those who advocate particular funds or opportunities for—for example—American minority students, in no way endorse lowering the competitive standards. Special funds are simply a question of keeping the pathways sufficiently open for critically important minorities at a moment when they are particularly narrow. The perception about some African students in applied fields, however, is that country needs have sometimes resulted in recruitment of candidates who would never be competitive in our own context. One faculty member stated quite vehemently that the stellar quality of African candidates from the 1960s cohorts had been very much altered by the urgency of "need" as the main criterion for choosing trainees. One creative way of mediating this problem has been to expand non-doctoral training to provide urgently-needed expertise. Most faculty would surely argue that creating a category of less-prestigious doctorates cannot possibly help the candidate, the country or the reputation of the field within U.S. scholarship. African Studies has had a high intellectual profile so far, and this is its greatest asset in the continued recruitment of such fine students; be they Americans of European ancestry, American minorities, foreigners, or Africans. The challenge now is to adapt its focus, not to alter its standards. Some realization of the problem may well already be helping to redress the situation. Certainly one knows of African students meeting extremely high standards in Africa-based research in technical fields.

At the doctoral level, then, there are some differences of emphasis amongst the pathways for training, and they must surely be very responsive to the funding priorities in the federal agencies, primarily USAID and the Department of Education. This overview of dissertation production—fraught as it is with methodological concerns—supports the inference that applied and technical studies have risen in profile over the past decade; that they have become predominantly African; that some progress has been made in attracting African students to the theoretical disciplines; and that this new wave of scholars has not been disproportionately placed in universities with area studies centers. As a result the total number of dissertations has continued to expand, and the total domain of scholarship about Africa has also diversified: in disciplinary emphasis, in composition by national origin, and in institutional dispersal.

Hence, part of the answer to how dissertation production could have continued to expand in spite of all recurrent fears about funding and jobs, is that a substantial and increasing proportion of students has been African, supported by special funding and focused on fields for which the U.S. job market is irrelevant. Another part of the answer has been changed career paths for Americans, into government and NGOs instead of academia. There is still an academic pathway for American students, but it is increasingly fraught by the indeterminacy of research funding, long training courses, difficult fieldwork conditions and uncertain futures. Funding clearly plays a critical role in shaping this demand.

The Funding of Doctoral Trainees for African Studies

American higher education is funded through a bewildering array of public and private institutions, most of which are beyond the influence of an Africanist constituency. Many students are supported by strictly competitive processes within their disciplines, that bear no relationship to the geographical area of their work. Fellowships from the National Science Foundation and the National Endowment for the Humanities, for example, are judged on merit alone. Some substantial quantum of training and research on Africa passes through these avenues, and in some disciplines Africanist work is particularly successful on merit grounds. Undoubtedly there are special sources for research and training in certain fields, such as religion, that also depend on internal criteria other than region.

Only in a very few places are students admitted into specifically Africa-focused programs (African Studies at Howard, African History at U. Wisconsin-Madison). Most are admitted into and educated in disciplines. On all issues of standards, from admissions to graduation and including the key funding decisions, students and faculty are under the authority of departments. Even where there are specific funds for Africanist students, such as the FLAS fellowships made available through Title VI, all of the fully-funded students submit to the funding criteria of departments and other agencies at critical transitions from stage to stage of their traineeships.

An examination of students needs to look carefully at each of the stages that make up the total traineeship, and the ways in which students move from one stage to the next. Most funding sources are particular to specific stages, so that the student has to make several transitions over the graduate career: admission, qualification for university funding (tuition and stipend), research funding, support during dissertation writing, and the job market. Most of them involve a fiercely competitive process and attrition of student numbers. In fact, one of the most difficult faculty responsibilities is to judge realistic drop-outs from avoidable losses to the discipline. Because these moments of transition are so sensitive, very small changes in the dollar amounts available can make very large differences and evoke very deep passions. In fact, the debates over student support could well be the basis for the famous comment that academic politics are so intense because so little is at stake. Debate about that "little" represents philosophical differences, internal maneuvering and disciplinary strategizing.

The Funding of Coursework

To maintain a high profile within American academia, any department within a university and any university within the higher education system has to be extremely competitive at one or another of these stages. Departments cannot admit and fund students at standards that differ widely from the rest of the university, and mean test-scores of applicants to universities become public knowledge. Some universities admit more broadly than they expect to graduate, thereby effectively endorsing student competition during the graduate years, on the assumption that only the survivors who have demonstrated commitment and ingenuity as well as ability will bring career credit to the institution. At the other extreme are a few universities (Stanford, Emory) that make admissions extremely carefully and then guarantee support for as long as four years, or even five (Chicago, for its best applicants in anthropology). This difference reflects philosophy and strategy, but also the university's general resource base, and its demand for teaching assistants (T.A.'ships) for undergraduate classes. T.A.s are the major means of supporting graduate students. Universities with a limited undergraduate teaching mission, or limited funding for augmenting help with large classes, will have few T.A. slots for graduate students.

Unlike the case in the sciences, doctoral students in our own disciplines are rarely recruited to carry out faculty research while being supported during the early years of training on faculty grants. Faculty grant-support may well be an as-yet unexploited resource for us as well, to supply

37

some student support at the research stage. But it will probably never figure in university calculations about how many funded slots to offer a department in the disciplines that make up Africanist research. Faculty ability to raise student support from their institution can be augmented above the university norm by competitive demand. The stronger the faculty, the greater their recruitability elsewhere, the better their case for extracting student support from the Graduate School if they decide to pursue this strategy. As in all else, the profile of the faculty matters.

The highest status programs in some disciplines—the University of Chicago in Anthropology is the prime example—have a structure that fosters attracting the most highly qualified students and giving them the best conditions of study. Some area studies centers at public universities, with less flexible funding, have particularly benefitted from the combination of tuition advantage, academic excellence and Title VI support to build the prominence and competitive edge they have: UC-Berkeley and UM-Ann Arbor in International Studies across the board, MSU in African development issues, Indiana in the African Humanities and Wisconsin in African history. Many excellent students come through other programs that have either solid funding or high disciplinary reputations combined with high student expectations of self-support. The result is a massive patchwork of admissions policies and funding conditions that shapes student recruitment, but always reflects in one way or another the competitive process by which American academia is structured: with respect to faculty profile and student support. Hierarchization of the field is explicit in all this, and will be exacerbated in the impending crunch over funding.

This decentralization of critical decisions about training, and the hierarchies that are created, means two things: that much of what goes on in most universities at the admissions and coursework stage is difficult to influence from the outside, but that small changes at key transition points may exert important leverage. It is the existence of a few FLAS fellowships per year, provided under Title VI, that gives the federally funded centers an advantage in recruitment and that allows faculties to generate various kinds of matching funds within the university. African Studies received a mean of 92 FLAS awards per year between 1985 and 91, or about 6—8 per center, including summer awards (CIE 1995:2).

The language-promotion policy that underlay the initial philosophy of Area Studies when it was founded in the 1950s still shapes in critically important ways the possibilities for training at the Title VI centers. Under the conditions of the FLAS fellowships, language study has to be taken every semester, which means that only students from a certain range of disciplines find it a desirable course to follow—anthropology, history, language and literature and political science—although political science was losing profile in area studies by the mid-1980s. The course requirements in other disciplines would never allow one fourth of all graduate class time to be devoted to language. When Title VI status is lost, the first thing to go is student language training, under the pressure of the cost of teaching minority languages, the disciplinary control over course requirements, and the desire of faculty and students for flexibility to respond to new training needs. Alteration of the language requirements for FLAS fellowships might alter the disciplinary profile of area studies considerably, but it would be very controversial. In fact, any major alteration of the FLAS system would have considerable reverberations for centers, disciplines, the expectations of research standards and the feasibility of linking new disciplines into the area studies/ international studies agenda.

The fellowships available to students shape the incoming "class," but the entire career-pathway of a student is influenced strongly by the availability of the entire spectrum of resources. If those are outside, competitive resources for the department or university, they play into the status/quality process that drives disciplinary agendas. Africa can come out very strong through its disciplinary bases if the students can tap into NSF, NEH and other funds that do not rest on area studies bases. Very small changes in the resources available from the interdisciplinary organizations such as area and international studies, however, can make one or other of the transitions of the "international/areas studies" graduate career either more inviting or more daunting, and add to or detract from the capacity of Africa to retain its profile.

Most interventions in funding for graduate study have been designed to preserve competition without allowing its mechanisms to eliminate all qualified people who come from important categories of the total pool, above all at a time when the selection pyramid is very steep. Funding for the early stages of graduate study for African-American and other minority students has generally achieved these conditions, and has therefore been far more welcome in African Studies than some commentaries imply. Almost all the programs that answered my request for information have some sort of minority fellowships. It has been remarkable, however, to find how consistently these fellowships mediate one hurdle but expect the student to be fully competitive at the next. For example, the Mid-West system (CIC fellowships) for minority students, provides two years of stipend but expects the university to waive tuition and the department to pick up the cost of further studies into the third and subsequent years. The overall pool of funds is therefore a factor from the outset, and a fully competitive situation sets in at the latest at the time of application for research funds. As far as I know, only the NSF, and only for the sciences, has a *research* competition that is ear-marked for under-represented American minorities.

As a result of the competitive structure for minority fellowships, I found faculty strongly endorsing minority fellowship programs because they expand diversity without altering standards. Unlike the case for fully-funded outsiders, the quality issue hardly arises. In fact, the director of one of the major programs regretted that competition for these fellowships was so stiff that in one of the major disciplines they had to turn down two well-qualified minority candidates in a single year, along—of course—with non-minority candidates.

In summary, then, the structure of graduate student funding should now "deliver" a set of ABD candidates that reflects the diversity of the pool of qualified initial applicants. Not all are securely funded on a multi-year basis, and relatively few are well enough funded to allow them to manage without taking jobs. But if the pool is good (a matter to be taken up later), the system may be a rickety Heath Robinson affair—in need of constant tinkering with the components and renovation on the curriculum side—but it works.

The Funding of Doctoral Research

The transition to doctoral research is more problematic. Here, on the whole, the African students are in much better shape than our own because of the Rockefeller ear-marked program (ADIA) and, of course, the AID-linked research. The others compete for a small number of opportunities, and if they fail two years in a row they either give up, change fields or take out loans to help them through. I was unable to come up with even an impression of magnitudes of indebtedness or the effects on attrition, but everyone knows of its existence and has a few horror stories to tell. It would be very interesting to know whether Africanists differ from others in their experience of what is said to be a growing general problem of debt in higher education.

The National Science Foundation, the National Endowment for the Humanities, the two Fulbright programs, and the JCAS of the SSRC/ACLS are the most important funding sources for research, although others include

AFRICAN STUDIES IN THE UNITED STATES

National Geographic, Rotary, and Wenner-Gren. The Africa component of NSF is hard to document, since the disciplines apply to different programs. The Fulbright program awarded approximately 60 graduate fellowships to Africa in 1992-93 (SSRC Assessment 1992). The Population Council gave two doctoral fellowships per year in recent years for research in Africa. Over the period 1980-87 an average of under seven dissertation fellowships per year were given to Africa by the SSRC/ACLS, rising to almost 15 between 1988 and 1992, but falling precipitously again as the external funding ran out (Szanton:1991, and supplement from SSRC).

It is worth noting that the Title VI African Studies centers were particularly successful in preparing their students for the SSRC competition. Between 1983 and 1989, 58% of awards went to those centers (Szanton 1991: 30). They accounted for just over half of the total applicant pool.

What do these resources for research funding add up to, relative to the numbers of trained ABD candidates in the pool for competitive funding? The applicant pool for the International Dissertation Research Fellowships of the SSRC in 1992 was 156 and in 1993, 145. Of these only 10 and 9, respectively, were funded (SSRC supplemental notes). Fulbright supports 60, and others in the academic category probably support a dozen or so more. We might come up with a generous conclusion, then, that 80 or so ABD students, coming from about 80 U.S. universities, get some kind of funding that can cover work in Africa. The rest must work with data sets, available documentary resources and Western-based interviewing (like Gingrich!), or drop out. Whatever the proportion of losses is, it must be high enough to account for considerable attrition. Recurrent crises in the funding of field research are disproportionately discouraging for the entire field. As I take up in Chapter 5, field research needs to be addressed as a topic all its own.

Overall, attrition and long-term languishing rates in our core disciplines are thought to be quite high. Anthropologists suggest as great as 50% loss, with a years-to-degree for the successful completers of between 8 and 9. With its field research component, African Studies is probably similar to anthropology. This sudden narrowing of the eye of the needle at the research stage, followed by very poor support for the period of dissertation-writing, followed in turn by struggle with the job market, represents the most discouraging phase of doctoral training.

AFRICAN STUDIES IN THE UNITED STATES

Synthesis

One can see from the funding picture that there are three pillars that support interdisciplinary doctoral training in African Studies, as distinct from the technical and purely disciplinary Study of Africa and the diffuse teaching of "things African" at all levels and in all venues. These are Title VI FLAS fellowships, the Fulbright Program and the JCAS of the SSRC/ACLS. The fourth and fifth pillars are the commitment of the universities and the scholars in African Studies to an interdisciplinary approach to teaching, and the cultivation of interdisciplinary networks for research. Reduction in two programs alone, the SSRC and the Fulbright, would reduce the research possibilities so drastically that I can only imagine an enormous clamor to expand the funds for NSF and NEH—which would then put a premium on disciplinary expertise rather than the interdisciplinary thrust that was one of the *raison d'être* of area studies programs in the first place.

The final topic that needs exploration is the reasons for student and faculty commitment to academic African Studies training, in the face of considerable fragility in the resources and the job market. There are only two plausible explanations. The first is commitment to Africa. Many students come in through undergraduate study-abroad programs and the Peace Corps. Even those who eventually leave academia and African Studies often still express a level of engagement that reflects the formative influence they feel the continent has had on their lives. Active involvement is a great creative force. The other reason is the intellectual challenge. There are still very bright students for whom Africa offers the inspiration they are seeking.

Doctoral Study in "The Study of Africa"

I review the AID-funded training of Africans in this country, not only for its own importance, but because the students make up a substantial part of higher education with respect to Africa.

The academic training of Africans in the whole roster of disciplines that make for development—from engineering to pharmacology—is a very large endeavor. The systems analyst for Human Resources Assistance at USAID generated the following table to summarize all African trainees in human resource projects, trained in the U.S., for FY 1985-FY 1995:

AFRICAN STUDIES IN THE UNITED STATES

Table 5:
African Trainees in the U.S., USAID Human Resources Development Assistance, FY 1985-FY 1995

Field of Study	Academic	Technical	Undefined	Total
Agriculture	1,668	4,029	0	5,697
Arts and Sciences	3,595	7,951	2	11,548
Business & Mnmt	990	5,484	2	6,476
Education	523	893		1,416
Energy	8	340		348
Environment	21	193		214
Forestry	86	139		225
Health	703	3,041		3,744
Population	63	777		840
Other/Unspecified	0	0	664	664
Total	7,657	22,847	668	31,172

Source: Cristina Mossi, Info*Structure* International.
(Note: The numbers include North Africa.)

Technical training predominates, but academic enrollments are very substantial. The vast majority from this program, however, have been in masters and professional training, rather than doctoral training.

Discussions at AID made it clear that doctoral programs have become very problematic for the funding agencies, with the exception of the elite ATLAS program whose grantees are very carefully and competitively picked by the country missions, whose full expenses are paid and 90% of whom successfully return after their training. For others, not only are there some misgivings about the length of time to finish, the relevance to Africa of the research and the difficulty of dealing with faculty, but the changes in the tax laws in 1986 meant that every visitor on longer-term training (with tuition coverage, annual stipends and so on) was in a high tax bracket for their support and had to submit extensive documentation. (I have heard the same story from visiting African faculty who were here before 1986 and after, and faced it with graduate students who were suddenly tax-liable for the "income" that tuition scholarships represented.) This provision clearly tips a balance of costs and benefits when an AID country-mission is considering a continuum of funding opportunities in training. They can choose between regular two-week in-country workshops for women entrepreneurs for several years, or one American PhD (this was the example given to me).

As a result, we begin to see a decline in African graduate students in this country. One of the responses to my letter mentioned that there was already a sense of the relative absence of Africans in the student body. The following table summarizes the changes in numbers of masters and doctoral students funded by AID programs, 1985-94.

Table 6:
AID-Funded African Students in the U.S., FY 1985-FY 1994 (includes Egypt)

	1985	1986	1987	1988	1989	1990	1991	1992	1993	1994
Masters	468	494	464	441	441	458	493	366	373	197
PhD	150	257	228	215	219	201	197	154	141	98

Source: Cristina Mossi, Info*Structure* International.

From a high of 751 in 1986, the numbers had fallen to 295 in 1994.

By far the greatest reductions have been in agriculture and arts and sciences disciplines. For simplicity's sake I tabulate the numbers for 1986 and 1994.

Table 7:
African Participants in all Training Projects in the U.S., 1986 and 1994, by Discipline

	1986	1994
Agriculture	627	377
Arts and Sciences	1,644	850
Business/Management	455	675
Education	133	216
Energy	6	29
Environment	1	68
Forestry	23	20
Health	381	282
Population	95	50

Source: Cristina Mossi, Info*Structure* International.

The shift in emphasis is quite marked towards business, education, and energy/environment.

AFRICAN STUDIES IN THE UNITED STATES

Discussion: The Problems of Students

The level of frustration with what the American PhD has become in the social sciences and humanities is widespread. It takes too long, costs too much, suffers too much attrition and interfaces too poorly with the job market as a result. At least, this is the view. An experimental Mellon-funded program at Michigan attempts to get history students through in six years. I came away from the research for this report convinced that in the coming phase of higher education we may see pressures to finish early and institute postdocs, after the pattern of the sciences. There is very little that African Studies can do about this except to think realistically about its own particular version of the problem: preparation for field research and time spent in Africa (see Chapter 5).

For the moment, there is still a demand from excellent candidates for the kind of training we offer. The social composition of the student body may well swing back to primarily American if the large funding agencies retreat from doctoral training. The funding rests on a narrow basis. Faculty and programs are bound to fear for the future.

My own sense, however, is that interests are also shifting *within* the disciplines in ways that we could be taking more into account. The rise in environmental studies, health and demography as components of the development endeavor will revive demand for culturally context-sensitive work in technical branches of ecology. The concern with human rights interfaces with law, and the mushrooming of NGOs creates interest in organizations and women's studies. One of our most theoretically-inclined colleagues is taking time out to retrain in public finance in order to carry out a research project. So the interdisciplinary agenda may well be on the verge of linking new disciplines to each other, and changing training programs quite radically in the process: to go beyond the achievements of connecting the classic core disciplines to one another, to put the contentious relationship with economics in perspective, and to reach out towards the sciences, management, and the professions.

4
THE INSTITUTIONS AND THEIR FUTURE

There are new pressures on all components of the funding picture in African Studies, although most are continuations of pressures that set in around 1980, or even before that, according to some sources. What is new this time around is the rhetoric of the dispensability of Africa that we find in public life. The end of the Cold War marked the end of an official public vision of Africa as serving American national interests: as a frontier with the Soviets and Cubans, and as a source of votes on key issues in the international organizations. The Somali crisis undermined the sense that quick military interventions could succeed without a cost in American lives; and for some, the Rwanda tragedy finished off all sense that even humanitarian aid could make a difference. Nine AID missions have been closed, and personnel and funds diverted to the former Soviet Union. One Washington authority conveyed to us that monies destined for Africa were diverted to pay for operations in Haiti; another knew that a state senator has been able to divert funds for Africa into a different endeavor at his home state university. An image is being created that most of Africa does not matter to the U.S. The term is "selective engagement."

We have yet to see how this will all work out. For the moment, and all threats to the contrary, funds that create opportunities within African Studies have survived. The Development Fund for Africa, founded in 1987, that earmarks about 800 million dollars, survived the recision bill in 1995. The many small funds that support scholarship and training are all under revision and many will be cut, but I have not yet found a case of total elimination even though most have been gradually notched down over a decade. The current exception is the SSRC fellowships, which are funded by foundations and appear to be in danger of total penury this year.

Particularly remarkable is the continuing support of universities. I was so surprised to find this pattern that I describe it first.

The Universities

The funding received by the National Resource Centers under Title VI of the National Education Act amounts to between $200,000 and $400,000 per center per year, reviewed competitively every three years. Several centers have received Title VI money for over twenty years, and have been able to use it judiciously to leverage matching and other funds from local resources.

AFRICAN STUDIES IN THE UNITED STATES

Guaranteed longevity has made it possible to dig in to the long-term tasks of building intra-university links. Anyone who has worked in a university knows how much work it takes to build up this kind of repertoire of resources:

• A Memorandum from CIE shows that a projected number of fellowships of 600 p.a. was turned into 800 by "the universities' willingness to supplement the Title VI funding, through tuition remissions, reduced tuition rates...or other funding sources."

• At Indiana, fee remissions are provided for instructors in African languages and for African Studies departmental teaching assistants by the College of Arts and Sciences, and fellowships were provided by the Office of International Programs (Title VI proposal 1994).

• At Michigan State, the largest African Studies Center in the country with an annual budget of $2.7 million dollars, "Considering all MSU support for Africanist personnel and activities, the ratio of MSU to US/ED support is more than 20:1." This counts faculty salaries, which are questionably a contribution to African Studies *per se*, but the breadth and complexity of their program is impressive.

• During the recent budget crisis at Berkeley, African Studies sustained reductions of only 13% as against the average level of 22%, and at Illinois-Urbana the administration "exempted the center from several rounds of budget cuts" (Title VI proposals).

• Florida-Gainesville has continued steadily to increase its African Studies faculty from 18 in 1978 to 52 at present, and is currently conducting an external search for a new director (which is always much more expensive than rotating an internal appointee). Illinois-Urbana conducted an external search in 1994-5, resulting in the appointment of Tiyambe Zeleza, and Northwestern in 1993-4 resulting in my own appointment. Since the new conditions and the new rhetoric were already in the public mind by then, these three appointments indicate the continued commitment of both private and public universities to investments in African Studies.

• Three HBCUs organized new undergraduate programs (Central State, Tuskegee and Lincoln), funded by Title VI. The University of Pennsylvania and three liberal arts colleges in the area (Bryn Mawr, Swarthmore and Haverford) created a joint African Studies program and had it funded for the first time in the present Title VI round (1994-7). Columbia was re-admitted to Title VI ranks, with an African-American, George Bond, as director. He joins Ed Keller at UCLA in the ranks of current African-American Title VI directors.

AFRICAN STUDIES IN THE UNITED STATES

• Universities have to cover full tuition for African students on the AID-funded AFGRAD/ATLAS program, and yet thousands of students have been trained in this country since the start of the project 30 years ago.

Why this willingness to invest in such a small field? Surely the fact that it meets several interests. Some of the Land Grant universities have benefitted from large AID support for development projects. African Studies and African scholars so substantially contribute to the goal of diversification of both faculty and classes that they pay off in the quality of university life. In a few places, African Studies is part of the university's claim to fame, with links to the long-term asset of a multi-disciplinary faculty, a magnificent library or a museum collection. Straight concern cannot be discounted as a motive in some places, for the development era. And due to their longevity and success, the African Studies centers have managed to diversify and adapt their portfolios, with a contribution here and a program there, with so many partners on the campus that they may simply enjoy goodwill and/or a capacity to keep assets away from systematic cuts. In my own work, I keep meeting people such as the representative of the Northwestern Alumnae organization who phoned me recently, who know hardly anything about Africa, but are very enthusiastic that we are here. Within some university communities we clearly stand out and are recognized.

Another explanation is that the universities are looking at student enrollments. According to *all* responses to my request for information on students, enrollments in undergraduate Africa courses remain high, and in many cases they close out. Enrollments do not seem to change much over time—to the surprise of one respondent. Another suggested that undergraduates respond only to the requirements and individual professors, not the world situation, and on both these counts Africa has retained a high profile. They warned against reading anything to do with a pre-existing and free-floating "interest in Africa" into the students' course choices, since interest is clearly created by the courses themselves. (I have not collected statistics on enrollments because of the well-warranted criticism of the Hamilton-Hodges report, by Jan Vansina, on the grounds that precise numbers are actually misleading. Ed Keller has compiled figures on the numbers of degree and certificate recipients, which may be more accurate). According to faculty reports of class enrollments in relation to their close-out levels, we are almost universally claimed to have remained very stable over the years, with brief peaks around remarkable events in Africa, such as the release of Nelson Mandela from prison. Harold Scheub must surely lead us all in this regard; he still teaches The African Storyteller to a closed-out course of 500 students every single semester at Wisconsin-Madison, and marks every paper and bluebook personally.

The interest of African-American students may be increasing. At the undergraduate level the same principles may apply: they are responding to the increased African-American and African faculty. At the graduate level, several letters indicated that the general effort to provide minority scholarships is beginning to show results, even though no such program—as far as I know—specifically targets African Studies. Some do target other disciplines such as the sciences and engineering, but on the whole the students themselves target their own interests.

I believe that continued support is also due to the quality of the work, both in teaching and research. The students of the "basic researchers" of the 1960s are now spread all over the academic scene, which must surely account for high quality work in so many places. It is very encouraging to see such a collective vote of support from our employers and students as a result. We are certainly poorer than in the heyday of basic research, and earning university support on the grounds of undergraduate teaching makes for an extremely time-consuming schedule that borders on incompatibility with research and even deep thought. But the infrastructure of faculty slots, library acquisition funds, student attendance and good will seems intact for the moment.

Fears are pervasive, however, that we are in a brief moment of respite before a blizzard of cuts, particularly at the public universities where I understand that legislatures want training to meet the manpower needs of the state, and are requiring the course loads and student ratios of the faculty to be high. They are actively promoting a constituency-accountability view of the educational mandate, which would probably diminish a focus on Africa except in communities with a large and vocal African and African-American pressure group. At some small private universities Africanists may well not be replaced when they retire, which will take a while, given the tenure system, but will eventually cut into the critical mass of scholars. In 1991 the National Council of Area Studies Associations published a report on faculty in all the area studies. Edna Bay reported that 17% of ASA members over 55 did not expect to be replaced upon retirement and a further 15% did not know what would happen (Bay 1991:18). Many thought that their position was basically the only non-western-society position in their department, and therefore might well go to a Latin-Americanist or a Sinologist.

Universities may also be worried about what are seen as developing trends within grant-making, towards expectations of matching funds from the outset. In the past, outside funds were used to leverage internal resources *after* the inception of the project, when there was already confidence in its future and resources to devote to the development of linkages. Trying to do this first requires different organization and a higher input by faculty and administration. A report on international studies developed at Wisconsin-Madison particularly notes the new challenges that matching funds put before the universities at a time of financial stress.

Universities change somewhat slowly, for both better and worse, because they are investing in processes of human capital formation that are cumulative, take time, and have to be planned in concert with a large number of other organizations. At the moment, the relatively deliberate turnaround time is very much in our favor in African Studies because it affords us a breathing space to do the new thinking necessary. Downsizing is probably inevitable, and should therefore be looked at as a challenge for regroupment. Judging by my collegial contacts in government and family contacts in business, we are in the very favorable position in academia of having this short grace period. As I have indicated throughout the report, this is a moment to use for creative reconstruction.

Government

The channels through which government resources flow into African Studies are numerous and varied: Title VI, NSEP, the Fulbright programs, USAID, and USIA, as well as whatever share for Africa is generated by particular individuals through a variety of other institutions such as The Smithsonian, NSF, NEH, NIH, and so on. They are all being reconsidered in light of Gore's "reinventing government" initiative and the current Congressional priorities. Nothing in the "big picture" bodes well for the level of Africa funding, but then many Africanist scholars have been critical of our past national engagements with the continent and might agree that things need changing. Again, it's a moment for focusing on the *content* rather than the *level* of activities alone.

AFRICAN STUDIES IN THE UNITED STATES

Title VI funding of National Resource Centers under the National Education Act (1980, but incorporating elements from the National Defense Education Act of 1958)

This is a bell-weather program for us in academic African Studies because it has supplied predictable funds (subject to competition for renewal every three years) for over thirty years. The basic structure is mandated; it comprises dependence on departmental faculty appointments for personnel and recourse to Title VI funds primarily for student support and programs, as well as certain elements of both training and programs. Language study is the most important component, and more recently outreach to the community, which now has 15% of the total budget devoted to it.

The following universities are now designated National Resource Centers in African Studies:

Boston University
Central State University (undergraduate only)
Columbia University
Howard University
Indiana University-Bloomington
Lincoln University (undergraduate only)
Tuskegee University (undergraduate only)
Michigan State University
Ohio State University and Ohio University
Stanford University
University of California-Berkeley and Stanford University
University of California-Los Angeles
University of Florida-Gainesville
University of Illinois-Champagne/Urbana
University of Kansas (undergraduate only)
University of Pennsylvania, with Bryn Mawr, Haverford and Swarthmore
                Colleges (undergraduate)
University of Wisconsin-Madison
Yale University (languages only).

There seems to me to be some misunderstanding of how area studies centers work within the university, which determines how the leadership in the field functions, why programs may go through cycles of activity and quietude, and the nature of the engagement with the disciplines. These are all

AFRICAN STUDIES IN THE UNITED STATES

phenomena that—in crisis—we tend to lay at the door of the field itself or even the region itself. Unlike departments, the Title VI centers as they were set up in the universities are not in control of the profile of their faculty. Every retirement or removal opens a space in a discipline; the replacement has to be recruited through departmental politics. The directors of the centers therefore have little power to plan to create clusters of scholars with common interests across disciplines. The best they can usually do is broaden the range of disciplines where African Studies is represented, or protect the status quo. A director hardly ever is in a position to attempt to recruit strategically, and can easily lose a star faculty member to a non-Title VI university because their discipline is stronger elsewhere. And where the directorship rotates, the programmatic strength changes over time.

Our relationship to the disciplines has meant that collaborative faculty in African Studies expect their operative networks to be somewhat dispersed, and to work on intellectual agendas through "invisible colleges." Thanks to our lack of emphasis on a foreign relations agenda during the Cold War period, we are not as extremely dispersed as a colleague in East European studies described their own situation to be; apparently not a single senior anthropologist of the former Soviet Union or Eastern Europe has been based at an area studies center. But we are not entirely concentrated either.

With respect to the current situation, then, African Studies faculties would not necessarily become more or less dispersed if Title VI were threatened, but they would stand to lose some of the *institutional assets* that have been leveraged from the sheer predictability of Title VI funding, at specific universities, in addition to the student fellowships, the language faculty (many of whom are not on tenure), and the community outreach. We all, as a community, would lose the centrality that the centers have been in the fostering of networks, which are the major form of intellectual organization: facilities for meetings, staff support for community outreach, the updating of libraries and databanks, etc. The University of Pennsylvania supports the World Wide Web database on Africa that was used by 84,000 people in the previous year. Indiana keeps a fine folklore archive. The Land Tenure Center at Madison preserves resources on land. Gainesville has specialist resources in tropical ecology. Columbia links into the international context of New York and the United Nations. Northwestern, a former Title VI center, has what is considered to be the finest Africana library in North America, if not the world. Michigan State, in addition to its intellectual strengths, has "loaned" the director, David Wiley, to compose position statements for public stands on behalf of the African Studies Association at various critical junctures. At this moment when assets are in short supply, we should be enhancing the capacity of centers to do the things they can do best with an eye to further fostering the links to international and other area studies.

We do not know what will happen to Title VI. The present cycle is funded through 1997, but the current government is expected to resort to recisions to cut federal fiscal commitments. There have been suggestions that the entire Department of Education should be closed down, since it is a recent creation from the presidency of Jimmy Carter. Administration of Title VI moved to Education in 1980, so there is no reason why it should not move again, in case of closure of the agency. Undoubtedly there will be vigorous lobbying for the preservation of a program which Lambert described as "taken for granted" but "if it did not exist we would be trying desperately to create it and at a cost that would be almost unimaginable" (1986:54). One alternative, however, might well be seen as a transfer of some of its functions to the Department of Defense, where a new program to support research and foreign travel was inaugurated in 1991 under the National Security Education Act (The Boren Act) of the same year.

The National Education Security Program

This brief review is based primarily on a circulated statement and other materials from David Wiley (1993), and by Professor Gwendolyn Mikell who served for a short time on the NSEP Board. My rendition is not their responsibility.

The content and purpose of the NSEP is uncannily similar to Title VI: "to lead in developing the national capacity to educate citizens to understand foreign cultures, strengthen U.S. economic competitiveness, and enhance international cooperation and security." "Backed by as much as $150-million in a self-perpetuating trust fund, the program is the largest new federal higher education project of its kind since the National Defense Education Act of 1958." It supports undergraduate scholarships, graduate fellowships and institutional grants (Desruisseaux 1993). The only innovations over Title VI appear to be links to business and engineering; business now has its own Title VI program. NSEP students are also required to work for the government in pay-back time for "not less than one and not more than three times the period for which the fellowship assistance was provided." The first grants under this program were slated to be awarded in 1994, for a total expenditure of $7.5 million.

AFRICAN STUDIES IN THE UNITED STATES

The organized African Studies community has opposed this program from the beginning, for the straightforward reason that it is located in Defense and there is a definitive presence of Defense and Intelligence employees on the Board. The motion of the Association of African Studies Programs urges simply that the program be transferred to Education (motion December 6th 1993, reconfirmed November 4th 1994). During the 1980s, Africanist scholars who supported U.S. policy (for example, in Angola, Zaire and South Africa) more or less withdrew from the African Studies community, which further solidified the divergence between policy-relevant and basic research. There has been considerable rapprochement, as I have argued already, but the NSEP may represent a new litmus test for the fissures in political commitment. According to NSEP officials, and the broader right-of-center community, African Studies maintains a greater distance from political engagement with our government than any other area studies community. It is hard to know, from the outside, where a dynamic such as this continues to be reproduced, or even whether it is true for government activities across the board as distinct from specific programs connected to intelligence.

The next stage in this drama will be played out over the coming months, and its resolution may have a definitive effect on the organizational infrastructures in area studies, including African Studies. For the moment, it is the future of NSEP that seems in doubt, rather than the programs run from Education.

The Fulbright Programs

Fulbright has been one of the pillars of funding for student and faculty visits to Africa since 1946. In the current round of budget cuts it has been saved ("by the White House"). Late last year a series of discussion papers was circulated about proposed changes. Like the other federal programs, changes would affect all area studies together, but unless there were special provisions for Africa, African Studies would be disproportionately affected because of the paucity of other funds.

On the table for discussion in the last round for which I have the documentation (May 1994) were cuts in the senior scholar program and the development of institutional grants. Binationalism was reaffirmed, as distinct from "a universal, worldwide program model;" that is, projects would be tailored to local agreements. The contentious provision here is a concern to combine the old criteria of competition and openness in the selection of senior scholars with new "standards" that would avoid making awards "which, to the layman, appear to support research that is purely for the academic and professional advancement of the individual researcher" (Fulbright Review Committee Second Draft, page 5). The theme of greater accountability for receipt of funds for scholarship, whether from government or other agencies, is a recurrent one.

This year Fulbright (Office of International Exchange) will fund 60-65 American students going to Africa (at about 12% of the total program budget, supported at the level of $18,000 each), 50 U.S. lecturers, and 23 researchers. The Institute for International Education will bring 376 African PhD candidates to the U.S. This constitutes about level-funding for the moment, but the expectation is for more drastic cuts by the current Congress than were envisaged with "reinventing government."

USAID

The funding that flows through African Studies from USAID has been voluminous and influential. In fact, the amounts are in a completely different category from the usual "Africanist" research (which typically costs between $50,000 and $100,000 for a senior scholar), even though universities and scholars figure in the consortia that are put together in response to Requests For Proposals. AID projects are multicountry and complex, comprising training, research, and implementation. For example, there is an RFP out now for projects to apply $50 million from the Development Fund for Africa, over seven years, to the problem of Equity and Growth through Economic Research (EAGER). The first two cooperative agreements are up for bid at $7 million and $5 million. Some of the funding goes to think tanks, some to NGO staffs, some to African trainees, and so on. Because of the complexity of this kind of program it may be difficult to predict how the coming changes would affect us in the training/research branch of the universities. Certainly particular scholars have recently brought in large grants to study democratization and the environment. And long-term cooperative agreements have produced basic research in some fields. Suffice it simply to note that the level of support is very high by comparison with any other concentrated discretionary funds in the academic study of Africa.

Rumors about the future organization of AID are coming out about once a week. The "reinventing government" initiative has already combined and re-sorted offices in ways that I ran across as I tried to collect documentation on the funding of training. Databanks have not altogether caught up with the titles of offices. On the other hand, a great deal is still going on. The AFGRAD/ATLAS program has been continuously funded for thirty years; a colleague in nutrition has been able to do absolutely seminal work in medical research under a cooperative agreement that has been in place since 1980; projects in Nigeria pushed on at least until December 1995, working through NGOs, under a partial waiver of the U.S. presidential decision to withdraw support for the Nigerian government.

In the immediate future the issues for us in the universities that will be more important than the total level of the AID budget for Africa are likely to be procedural. First, my discussions of training with AID officers revealed an increasing dissatisfaction with the academic PhD in this country. It takes too long, is too expensive, indeterminate in outcome and only contingently related to in-country needs. Whatever one thinks of this judgement, it adds another voice to the growing chorus of concern about the PhD course of study. Many AID-funded trainees now take other kinds of courses of study, some of them outside the university system altogether.

Secondly, the conditions of the EAGER project contain even stronger accountability standards than are proposed for the Fulbright program. The strictures with respect to publication could not be followed by an academic without modification because they affect freedom to publish. One understands that such modifications are managed. But again, the principle and its implementation have to be faced with respect to the agencies who would become African Studies' most important clients in a constituency-oriented model of research and training.

USIA

Again, there are many programs that can—or could if they were used—benefit the university community: Citizens Exchange, International Visitors, and College and University Affiliations Program. The federal government has altogether 23 agencies involved in international exchange. Citizens Exchange requires matching funds that may be difficult to manage for universities, and International Visitors requires a lot of logistical work. We probably do not use these programs as much as we could.

Between 1982 and 1994, the University Affiliations project funded 20 exchanges, with budgets ranging from $50,000 to $124,000. This year the program received 46 applications, of which "about half were very presentable," but only 2 or 3 will be funded. I don't know whether this represents a reduction from times past. Nor have I had time to explore the full range of exchange programs run by USIA. But as an indicator of demand and supply it suggests that in the area of exchange we may be funding about 10% of the quality-level interest at this point.

Summary

The federal government permeates the funding of area studies and is particularly important in African Studies since the continent cannot meet the U.S. half way in scholarship and exchange, as can Western Europe and the Far East. Most programs are already highly competitive; others would require innovation within academia to accommodate them, especially considering the other pressures on university funding, faculty time and our standards for publication. The pressures on the budget and the concerns for constituency accountability (whatever that turns out to mean) will therefore be all the more important to us in the future.

Key Africanist Organizations

The African Studies Association (ASA)

The ASA was founded in 1957 as an organization of individual dues-paying scholars, from all disciplines, whose work focuses on Africa. The membership grew rapidly in the early years, and considerably again in recent years. It was stable at about 1,400 from 1972 until the late 1980s (actually, two sources on the growth in membership are discrepant), and now stands at about 3,230. The executive office moved from UCLA to Emory University about five years ago. The full-time position of executive secretary has turned over recently. The Association runs a variety of activities, services and publications, the most important of all being the annual conference at which about 600 papers are given, to a total attendance of about 2,000. The African participation rises every year. Papers are given by members of an ever-widening array of organizations. Often the conference is carried in the African press.

Alongside this growth has gone a reinstatement of controversy and multiple constituencies after a long period of retreat from engagement. In

AFRICAN STUDIES IN THE UNITED STATES

Montreal in 1969 there was a serious confrontation between the executive board and the Black Caucus, centering on the representation of African and African-American scholars in the organization and on the engagement of the Association with issues of crucial relevance to them. A detailed review of this critical event is provided in Challenor (1969). Three years later the following statement was made to the Board by the executive secretary: "the Association is not engaged, as it was formerly, in discussions and exchanges with foundations, agencies, institutions, and other associations, nor is it engaged seriously with the African Studies programs in the United States." (Executive Secretary Duffy, quoted in Bay 1991:4). Only by the mid-1980s was the ASA led away from the insularity of the past almost-20 years. A key turning point was the invitation to return made to important members of the African Heritage Studies Association (formerly the ASA Black Caucus) when Robert Cummings was ASA President in 1985.

One has the impression that like all elective bodies the Board is comprised of members who have a range of commitments and levels of work. Institutional memory and sustainability of effort are always at issue when the turnover in board membership is three years, and in the leadership, two years (shorter than the SSRC committee). Initiatives can be hard to maintain if the Queen Mary has to be turned round every couple of years. Race recurs as an issue at the meetings, although there is now a much wider range of opinion within all constituencies, as well as between the racial categories. Disagreements have recently been vociferous, for example, between those in favor and those against reparations for slavery, and between those who speak from Africa and those who speak from African-America (see Taiwo 1995, for example, for a critique of Gates and Appiah). The annual forum of the conference offers the usual mix of any academic meeting. Everyone expects it to be part performance, part marketplace, and above all (as Clifford Geertz wrote of markets in general) a focus for the communication of all manner of information.

As an elected membership organization, the ASA can only be what its bylaws and the vigor of its board, president, and executive secretary allow it to be. All but the executives are non-paid volunteers. Its legal status precludes lobbying, so all political pressures for professional causes or African issues have to be organized through networks. More activist work is organized through three affiliated mechanisms: a board committee on current affairs, the Association of Concerned African Scholars which has been oriented primarily to South Africa, and *ISSUE: A Journal of Opinion*. Many members organize their own networks for civic causes.

Most members are pretty realistic about what an organization such as the ASA can be, and it certainly has fulfilled critically important mandates as our largest membership organization within these limitations. Current revitalization includes an endowment campaign.

The Joint Committee on African Studies of the Social Science Research Council and the American Council of Learned Societies (JCAS/SSRC-ACLS)

The importance of the JCAS is that it represents not centers or card-carrying members but networks; and networks are our most creative form of social organization. The committee consists of about eight or ten scholars, usually at the associate or full professor level, who are chosen to serve terms of about five years. The criteria include the need to represent the full breadth of the field in both disciplinary and social/ethnic terms. Unlike the Executive Board of the ASA, which is elected, the JCAS maintains a continual balance, in spite of the turnover in membership. Each member accesses their own networks for input, and the relationships amongst the committee members can form critically important interdisciplinary networks for the future. Give and take certain moments, then, I would say that the JCAS accesses the breadth of good thinking in African Studies, and is highly respected.

Over the years there have been strong criticisms about the composition and inclusiveness of the committee. But to the degree that these come from real constituencies in the field, they have been a force for modification of committee practise. During my own term on the committee (1981-86), a major challenge was launched regarding the inclusion of African-American networks in committee projects. After the confrontation at Montreal in 1969 the new scholars joining the ranks of the Africanist professorate straightforwardly expected to take part in all activities, regardless of "identity" criteria of any kind. There was some agony at the time that this issue should need to be addressed yet again, but it was addressed, since the mutual withdrawal of the 1970s must surely have been very much worse. Friction is an inevitable concomitant of intimacy: abrasive, unpredictable with respect to target, timing and reason, but inescapable. And there were other sources of friction as well, including philosophy towards current intellectual and political issues and approaches to feminism, not to mention personality factors. As a member of JCAS, however, I learned something about the interpersonal politics and enormous intellectual potential of area and international studies in a uniquely stimulating way, and created working relationships with co-members and others that continue to shape my professional life. I assume that service on the committee has had the same effect for others. Since then, the committee has changed as well. After a series of extremely good "white male" chairs from the social sciences, the past chair was an African from the humanities (Anthony Appiah) and the current chair is an African-American woman, currently serving as a director of international studies (Pearl Robinson).

The JCAS has only ever given out a few doctoral fellowships a year, as described in the previous Chapter. Its importance far outweighs the numbers. First of all, the fellowships have been very competitive and therefore highly prestigious within academia. The stress on field research helps to institutionalize this, our most important, methodological foundation. And the interdisciplinarity has done a great deal to alter the narrowness of training at the graduate level.

Since its other activities are shaped by the visions of committee members about where we should be going, the committee has also produced very inventive and viable ideas. The research overview papers that were commissioned throughout the 1980s cost about $1,000 each in honoraria but they produced a set of resources that truly attempted interdisciplinary thinking, and that have been used far outside African Studies. Several of them opened up whole new topics, and a few have been turned into books. One—Mudimbe's *The Invention of Africa*—became a classic. The series was ended after ten years. One of its wholly unintended consequences had been to reinforce the library-based tendency of the 1980s, and the relative delegitimation of experience-based knowledge. The new series of commissioned Explorations papers will avoid this trap, and at the same time address the new issues arising out of globalization. Several other very valuable activities have arisen out of members' particular interests: a project supporting the infrastructures of African museums, workshops in Africa on agricultural research, a conference on material culture, a series of activities on fertility, and so on.

The quality that all these projects have in common is the endorsement, at relatively low cost, of the vision of committee members of the "creative next step," around which they mobilize their own networks. In the view of one participant and commentator we did much less well when we tried to create thematic competitive fellowship projects, in response to the current interests of funding agencies. The themes ended up over-directing the research agendas of individual scholars. Applications were lower quality, returns were less satisfying, projects needed shaping but nevertheless proved recalcitrant, and so on. In a program for individual research, choice of topic was better left to applicants, so that judgment about funding could rest straightforwardly on criteria of quality.

The thematic interdisciplinary research of the present stage of area studies work was really trailblazed by the JCAS, but with mixed results. A further shift towards constituency-orientation will have to be thought through even more carefully. It is not always possible, for reasons to do with criteria for disciplinary judgement, to get the best research by setting the topic from the outside. Research is our coinage, and it doesn't do well in the authenticity/originality stakes when mixed with too much else. Given an over-focused research topic, a good scholar will always move to master its limits, not stay within them. The finest scholarship will gravitate to the NSF and other remaining non-directive peer-review contexts. There should be no reason, however, why a chosen topic should not bring out very high quality work if the activity is a workshop series, an overview paper, an exchange or a training program, as long as the specific composition remains substantially at the organizer's discretion. Funders' use of the competition system would presumably then be the means of matching their own agendas with those of the grantee, as has always been done.

The current SSRC international programs have become financially problematic. A new policy will not be fully articulated until the new president's policies are chosen. Under David Featherman, and in line with the universal cost-cutting efforts, a plan was developed for reorganization of the area studies programs that would be both cost-effective and ensure that global issues would not fall between the cracks of the "areas." It was suggested that committee composition should reflect "the ability of individuals to contribute to scholarship on issues of particular relevance" (Heginbotham Memorandum 1994:15), which represents an attempt to come to terms with thematics by reorientating the agendas represented by the area committees as they presently exist. This plan was not implemented but the issues it addressed are still relevant.

The most damaging development would be the limitation of dissertation fellowships below the critical number that keeps the students hopeful and working. At a certain point the odds must seem to them too long to bother. Far more is lost at this critical threshold than the dollars saved can ever measure. In the early 1980s the committee members worked in every spare moment to try to augment the numbers above a handful, including developing the first thematic project: on African Agriculture, Crisis and Transformation (of which I was an organizer, along with Michael Watts, Pauline Peters and Sara Berry). Now they seem to be back in the same situation.

This is all very discouraging and provokes defensive thinking rather than innovation. I would argue that one of the best investments in African Studies would be to have the present committee draw up a multi-year plan of transformation for itself, towards a particular set of goals and in light of the internationalization agendas, negotiate a budget and fund it. It should not be a fund simply to sustain the same kind of activities as in the past, successful as these have been, because in the near future we will not be living under the same conditions. The present chair is the right person to mediate it, and there is no other organization that has so consistently enjoyed the confidence of the community.

The African Heritage Studies Association

The AHSA was founded by the ASA Black Caucus following discussions about "their common plight" within the ASA. The central concern was "to cater to black scholars and to correct the teaching of Euro-Africa rather than Africa in the U.S. colleges and universities" (quoted in Rowe 1970:4). Always Pan-African in orientation, the first meeting in June of 1969 and first major conference in 1970 included scholars from Africa and the Caribbean as well as the U.S. The AHSA separated from the ASA after the Montreal meeting in 1969, and became the primary professional association of several important African-American scholars specializing in Africa. Some have returned to the ASA as fully active participants; other have not, on the grounds that the ASA has not sufficiently changed over the intervening 25 years. Some members go to both meetings. In addition to an annual conference, the AHSA publishes a journal twice a year, The *International Journal of Africana Studies*, and a thrice-yearly Newsletter.

The Association of African Studies Programs

This organization was founded in the 1970s by the directors of the Title VI programs to address collective concerns. It is a membership organization that has long since affiliated even very small programs at small colleges. There are about 70 member programs. It works in the small budget made up from the dues. The leadership works on the activities as part of their professional commitment.

There are a few organizational duties that the AASP takes on, such as the collaborative distribution of resources and students for the summer language programs in African languages, to avoid duplication. The membership passes motions on political issues that directly affect the relationship between the federal government and program resources. For example, the meeting passed a motion requesting the removal of the NSEP program to the Department of Education. This year the membership explored the possibilities for encouraging linkages with the HBCUs. Where African Studies programs do not exist in those institutions, deans were invited to our last meeting in Washington.

The directors of programs meet in Washington in the spring, to catch up with the federal programs that fund exchanges, research, internship opportunities for students, and so on. In 1995 there were presentations by staff for both political parties and for the Congressional Black Caucus. George Moose, the Under-Secretary of State for Africa, attended for about an hour and a half. The Association does not organize political or civic engagement around Africa issues, but it does maintain an active Washington connection.

Disciplinary Organizations

It is worth noting briefly that all African Studies faculty belong to their disciplinary organizations as well, and switch their energies back and forth according to how stimulating the debates are, how useful the networks to their students, and how important the funding sources. This is very important for the liveliness of the area studies associations. The "endorsement" of a few major scholars who come to the meetings, publish in the journals, work for area studies committees and generally validate the field, cannot be overstated. The U.S. academe does work, at the top of the hierarchy, on a "star system." There have been periods during which senior Africanist scholars in the disciplines have consistently failed to attend the ASA annual conference, which then makes it less important for their students to attend...and so on. At moments of stress such as we are now in, the two agendas of addressing the larger popular constituency and addressing the particular expectations of university and discipline are in direct competition for limited time and energy.

AFRICAN STUDIES IN THE UNITED STATES

Foundations

I limit my observations to a few points that shape our own perceptions at present. The foundations have supported African Studies with enormous generosity intermittently over its entire history. What we see now are a much higher level of competition for funds and a more vigorous setting of agendas. In part I think this must result from the increased range of philanthropic organizations on the American scene. The radicalism of the later 1960s seems to have inspired the formation in the early 1970s of many explicitly conservative foundations oriented to developing different agendas within higher education. In the 1980s, the beginnings of the retreat of government from social issues set in, and the foundations were asked to pick up the slack. As many have argued, the concern for relevance began to exert a stronger influence on decisions.

With respect to Africa, the most obvious sign is regional demarcation for funding. Of the seven foundations that explicitly list Africa as a priority in the Foundation Directory, four mention only Southern Africa (The International Foundation, Kellogg, Mott and the Rockefeller Brothers), Carnegie mentions both Africa and Southern Africa, and the remaining two are the familiar Ford and Rockefeller Foundations. Obviously many others do support Africa initiatives under thematic programs. But the impression is clearly conveyed that there is no specific funding constituency for Africa, as there is for Japan, China, Western Europe, Eastern Europe (Soros) and probably others. The wealthy of Africa do not support scholarship very much, and the business community in this country is not committed deeply enough to earmark endowment funds. The oil companies have funded exhibits on Africa, but we may never have been aggressive enough with them to extract a commitment to scholarship.

The financial weakness of Africa and African interests puts scholarship in a weak situation if the watershed in intellectual life is leading towards constituency-oriented work, a topic to which I now turn briefly.

Constituency-Oriented Research and Training

It seems to me incontrovertible that we are heading in this direction. During the 1980s more and more social research was done under contract, and we now find the old sources of funding—the government and foundations—being more directive. NGOs are branching out into research. Universities have to follow the funding to keep the books balanced. The era has gone when the founders of international and area studies in this country created the field, defined the agenda and commanded the resources. The works they produced may stand as the traditional canon, but they are not reproducible except by the brilliant individualist who decides to throw career caution completely to the winds. (It has been done, to great effect!) On the negative side, David Wiley has referred to this as "the new world of commercialized scholarship," which is likely to entail "the tendency to set aside academic values" (1993:4).

Before leaping one way or the other, we need to look at the issue historically and broadly. After all, many of our own people have argued in favor of relevance; Mamdani's (1990) critique of U.S. scholarship was based on a commitment to engagement with the struggles of African people for a decent way of political and economic life. In her rejoinder Pearl Robinson (1990) suggests a search—both analytically and socially—for a position that is neither silent nor consensual. While the independence of scholarship is a basic credo, the "ivory-tower" quality of some academic work of the 1980s was not necessarily produced by conviction so much as by the reprise of the disciplines in a very tight job and resource market. At one extreme lies total self-direction and at the other a completely unacceptable capitulation to frankly interested work. There are other viable positions in between.

How a constituency-orientation model might work depends entirely on who is defining what kinds of work, and how that relates to the maintenance in one form or another of the inherited asset of guild standards. The saying about pipers and tunes to the contrary, in the life of artistic and professional expertise the nature of the tune is at least deeply influenced by the vision of the artist. Many great artists would prefer to work in penury, or give up altogether, than play something that is simply dictated to them. There is going to be no easy answer to this dilemma, and all kinds of parties will have input before rubrics emerge. A small field like African Studies, that will be dependent on a few sources if it is to function on anything more than the considerable commitment of its members, should be a place to engage in the conversation and to experiment with solutions. In my own view there should be productive new possibilities in the match of expertise to issue and constituency, but it's a departure and should never upstage the kind of work that only academics do: extended empirical projects on the long-term process of social and cultural life, with a view to analytical critique and the creation of new interpretations and new visions.

AFRICAN STUDIES IN THE UNITED STATES

In this short moment for reflection before the forces I have outlined in Chapter 2 set in with greater strength in African Studies, we should take the time to look at the possibilities and contribute creatively to the setting of some key agendas for the immediate future. As I will discuss at the end of Chapter 4, I'm not sure that we have the right kinds of organization to achieve this debate, just as we seem to be lacking a group that can lobby on our behalf in the political arenas.

5
DEBATES AND CHALLENGES

Area Studies and/or International Studies

America is the prototype of the diasporic "pluribus" community of the future. Most urban children attend schools in which twenty or more mother tongues are represented amongst their classmates. Dollars and trade are everywhere. Millions subscribe to National Geographic. And yet there has been a recurrent panic, about every ten years since 1945, about how to overcome our "insularity." The present concern for internationalization of research and curricula is a replay of concerns expressed in very similar terms in the immediate post-World War II period, the post-Sputnik era, the early 1970s and the early-to-mid 1980s.

It is impossible to look at the debate about the future of one of the area studies without devoting a couple of paragraphs to this anomaly, because the specific terms in which the issue arises this time around and the reasons why solutions obviously did not "work" before, will affect us all. In the mid-1980s there was a concerted attempt to create a National Foundation for International Studies, on a par with the NSF and NEH. It did not succeed, for reasons I have not had time to explore. The argument in its favor, entitled *Points of Leverage* (Lambert 1986), offers a remarkable view of the strengths, overlaps and gaps in the U.S. engagement with the rest of the world. I read it in 1995, at a time when the U.S. is pulling resources out of the U.N., and in conjunction with an African colleague's commentary on his own impressions of a U.S. academy that recoils from sustained critique of "central terms of reference...and key animating debates."

The claim that Americans do not know or care about the rest of the world must be, in part, an official stance to allow selective engagement to look plausible. Claims of insularity have also allowed an evasion of engagement with the arguments of world systems theory which were so influential in the academy in the 1970s and 1980s. But the American population is surely not so much insular as intransigently bilateral and optative. Global knowledge and global theory are avoided because each constituency can withdraw from most of it most of the time, if they wish. On the other hand, groups within society intensely cultivate detailed local knowledges: places of origin, centers of economic partnership, beauty spots for vacation, political and religious networks for the pursuit of common agendas, and so on.

The institution of area studies in the 1950s was justified in a very interesting way: not as a corrective to a failure on the part of society at large, but to a failure of the academic *disciplines* to incorporate international knowledge. If there is a single theme throughout the ensuing debates it is the continuation of that failure. Lambert writes in 1986 that "Economics and sociology, two disciplines that one might have expected to be heavily represented in language and area studies, are opposed as a matter of faith" (1986:63). In African Studies we have a special program (the pre-dissertation field-study awards) to try to get around the disciplinary barriers, but a colleague wrote to me that the disciplinary lock on academic jobs, in a very competitive job market, makes the work to acquire area specialization an unattractive and expensive proposition. In his overview of the present state of play in international and area studies, the vice president of the Social Science Research Council implicitly sees the area studies institutions as being called on to adapt more fundamentally than the disciplines to the new situation of the post Cold War world; for example area studies scholars and centers will focus "*more than in the past* on training scholars and practitioners who *specialize within disciplines* to understand..." (Heginbotham 1994:37, my emphasis). Read as part of a history, this represents realism, rather than principled conviction, about disciplinary strength.

Why, however, have the disciplines been so successfully recalcitrant that Lambert could write: "After 30 years of federal support for campus-based international studies, we are still in the 'pilot project' stage" (1986:4)? The answer may not be possible to define, but it matters very deeply to pose the question, because otherwise the failure will be laid at the feet of area studies scholarship, in the context of another effort at internationalization and the inevitable competition for resources. First of all, not all disciplines are the same; history, anthropology, language and literature have context-sensitivity built into the disciplinary structures. Their own challenge—and one they have themselves seen for at least ten years—is to develop ways of studying multi-site phenomena with the same sensitivity as they have studied times and places. I can only imagine us all embracing the new opportunities for this kind of work that resources in International Studies would offer. Area studies has already fundamentally altered at least some of the scholarship in these core disciplines over the past thirty years: anthropology has become historically inflected, historians study narratives and diaries, and literature draws on the work of Clifford Geertz. Political Science has bordered on the interchange a little more cautiously; geography has engaged fully but in small numbers; a successful Rockefeller Foundation project brought area studies scholars and agricultural scientists together. In the core disciplines, then, area studies has already done some of what Heginbotham is suggesting, by dint of great effort and in the teeth of some inertia from within the disciplines. In a content-analysis of the *African Studies Review*, Sanders writes: "change and growth in the journal have been guided more by changes in disciplines than by efforts to re-direct or change African Studies. The only exception to this might be the synthesis articles solicited through the SSRC" (1993:124). The authors of those overview papers were carefully chosen to represent the most forward-looking work. So there is a leadership that should be enthusiastic about adding the new agendas.

The problem lies not in what *has* been done in area studies, but with what has *not*. Some disciplines have not participated to anything like the same degree, and most notably academic economics, as Heginbotham goes on to say, by way of an example: we need training "to understand how the culture, history, and language of a local context shape its interaction with, for example, the evolution of market institutions and engagement with international market forces" (1994:37). If the main problems for internationalization are economics and the professional schools perhaps it would be worth simply stating that, and proceeding from there. Again, this should be welcomed by those of us who labor in the disciplines and area studies, because we have very deficient technical training to trace out the implications of the economic forces that affect everything we study (see, for example, my edited collection on money; Guyer 1995). I am optimistic that an international studies infrastructure could, in fact, achieve this. The reality of vast populations not linked into the banking system at all, of exchange rates in what Collier terms "small open economies" (1994) that are extremely vulnerable to speculative forces, will surely attenuate the hold of an economics that is unnecessarily universalistic in its theoretical claims. The global political economy is one of several topics—along with migration, the communications media, and violence—that cannot be taken on by area studies alone. We need international studies, and certainly should not be pitted against it, as if we had failed in the mission to internationalize (all) the disciplines and now needed to be superseded. The disciplines themselves still need to embrace theoretical and susbtantive inspirations that come from the international world.

The very considerable advantage of being precise about a) the power of the disciplines to contain the influence of area studies and set the conditions of work, and b) the very particular power of economics to opt out altogether from the beginning, is that we do not now identify failures with the area studies establishment itself (the SSRC committee, the Title VI Centers, Africanists in general), as some seem to want to do. We stand to undermine

71

invaluable resources, with no guarantee whatsoever that they would be replaced at all, let alone by something better.

Before moving on, I want to ruminate about the effect of computer technology in some disciplines versus others. Over the past fifteen years economics and political science have embraced modelling, and if they move into intellectual space afforded by international studies, we who specialize in "context sensitive" research (to use Pearl Robinson's term) need to envisage some form of collaboration. I have been convinced that this is potentially a good thing: by difficulties in my own research and by listening to natural scientists describe how modelling has allowed formerly unimaginable cross-disciplinary work on complex ecological systems. But it may need managing in order to be maximally fruitful and to avoid such eventualities as the total takeover of the agenda by the single discipline of economics, as happened, for example with the journal *Economic Development and Cultural Change*, which was started by anthropologists and is now entirely economics; or (as I understand it) with the near-complete scoop of new NSF money for environmental studies by economists. If this happened—as it could, without the link to a strong and continuing area studies tradition— international studies and area studies would simply become a new incarnation of the two sides of the old and dire opposition between quantitative and qualitative research, between universalizing and particularizing disciplines. The logic is a strong one. International Studies, as a forum for coming to grips with global forces, could well become a staging ground for the same universalizing economics that avoided engaging with area studies in the past.

Area studies might then become what it already is edging towards: the academic incarnation of our national bilateralism, where each area belongs to its own constituency and generates a form of local knowledge, by, for and about "the people." It almost goes without saying that I think this would represent another lost opportunity in the apparently endless quest for genuine internationalization of American scholarship. It can be that, and to some degree should and certainly will be that, as national life becomes more and more privatized. But both endeavors can be much more if they are not pitted against one another, or mutually accommodated through a simple but intellectually negative disciplinary division of labor between economics and political science on the one side and history and anthropology on the other.

What better possibilities are there? The increased possibilities for comparison and the study of global forces that an International Studies infrastructure offers are only one step forward. The real opportunity for both is a vigorous expansion of the interdisciplinary frontiers that became rather cemented in the "core disciplines" approach of the area studies tradition. Our most strategic resource is the small cadre of younger economists, political scientists and specialists in climate change, remote sensing and international migration, who know both some area studies and modelling techniques. They are our first cohort of scholars to be methodologically polyvalent, convinced of the importance of context-sensitivity and also ready to address some of the analytical and philosophical issues that my African colleague pointed out. To have made it through the disciplinary ranks under present conditions is a tribute to their talent rather than to any conviction about the value of contextual work on the part of the disciplines.

It matters very much, then, which elements—disciplines, and scholars within disciplines—become the brokers under a new dispensation of international and area studies. At several universities African Studies specialists have taken on the job of managing international studies centers, precisely with a view to preempting the EDCC scenario. Most of the technical expertise, however, is still more junior that this. We also think that there are African counterparts, but they show up topic by topic rather than as a particular cohort, especially since the African academic context does not foster their affiliation with "Africanist" organizations. In my own view, these people need particular support to define an interdisciplinary agenda that would include both sophisticated model-building/quantification and the context-sensitive definition of variables and reading of findings without which the whole exercise can be meaningless. This is an "interdisciplinary" task that we have still not, after all these years, really taken on. For both area studies and international studies, there are new disciplines that need to be inter-related with one another in order to address the fundamental intellectual problems. It should be noted here that much of this work is "relevant" in the developmental sense. It relates to environmental change, agricultural development, public finance and the culture of democratization— all topics that lend themselves readily to international comparisons.

Are we addressing the issue of international studies within African Studies? Yes, but piecemeal in particular works within specific networks, by preempting the reprise of an IR or macro-economics control of leadership positions, and through the work of individual scholars (notably several of the African faculty who came here in the 1980s). The interest of major universities in appointing Africanists to these positions reflects a vote of confidence that they as individuals and our own traditions of thinking about international issues represent a promising way forward; we are certainly not holding these positions by virtue of the intrinsic importance of Africa to U.S. foreign and economic policies. We are still in the first stages of their directorships, so the intellectual thrust they may be able to give is not yet bearing fruit. The future of an intellectual presence lies with the ways in which junior faculty can make use of the space both area studies and international studies opens up. Judging from past experience, the real challenge will be to foster as solid an interdisciplinearity amongst other disciplines as areas studies has created amongst its own core disciplines over the past thirty years. As long as the framework of international studies fosters this, both international and area studies can only gain from one another.

The Social and Intellectual Composition of African Studies

In our collective contexts more attention is being paid to the need—in our own case a pressing need—to create the kind of bilateral/constituency support that other areas benefit from that I bring up next. In the newly privatized world of the 1990s, it is both a pragmatic and moral challenge to promote African-American participation and leadership; if Africa and African Studies decline in profile it will definitely not be because of the intellectual marginality of the work but because of simple lack of "relevance" to enough U.S. citizens.

All area studies in this country have potential self-selected constituencies, by ethnic origin. They may or may not be interested in scholarship, and they may have their own idiosyncratic interests within it (esthetics, for example, ancient history, or religious studies). Their ordinary lives predispose them to engage. Most area studies include scholarship by immigrants from the area and members of the ethnic constituency. The resulting inter-ethnic interface of non-national and national scholars must be one of the most productive assets of the area studies format: there's no escaping one another, in the day-to-day confrontations with ideas, students, administrators and the currents of political change. The study of one group by another, indefinitely, bypasses all kinds of important intellectual possibilities that constant engagement fosters. And if bilateralism is the dominant form of American internationalism, this kind of exclusiveness is also unsustainable over the long term.

I don't know of any reliable way of estimating the African-American presence in the African Studies professorate, but it must be higher than it was. As far as I know no white scholar in African Studies is explicitly opposed to increasing the proportion of Africans and African-Americans in the ranks beyond the level it has now reached. In my own experience the debates are about three issues that immediately arise once the composition of the community has been altered: authority (scholarly and institutional); access to resources; and the inclusiveness of networks, including most importantly the networks through which the field is reproduced. Such issues strew blood and feathers on the academic floor regardless of who the parties are. Undoubtedly the confrontations are further embittered when race enters in. But my own impressions have been so favorable about the possibilities for maintaining engagement, not least due to the generosity of our African-American colleagues, that I would certainly not see the field as polarized or engaged in unresolvable struggles.

Three illustrations must suffice: the institutional dispersal of African and African-American studies after the mid-1960s; the competition for academic jobs, resulting in a perception by some of a "ghettoization" of African history, which is the discipline that is hardest hit by the job crunch; and the problem of scholarly authority and the published

"canon." i) During the 1960s, the changed racial profile of the student body and the raised social consciousness on campuses gave rise to a struggle to address African-American intellectual concerns. The main concern, of course, was that the canon was implicitly or explicitly racist. Those of us who were students then can certainly attest, for example, to the pervasiveness of reference to "primitive societies," in the very presence of students from those societies. Evolutionary paradigms were only just beginning to shift. And only in certain contexts was scholarship beginning to address social movements as making positive contributions to justice and equality. Area Studies had arisen in a critical stance vis-a-vis the disciplines, which were seen as being quite intransigently authoritative in their own western style, so some area studies scholars were not necessarily as quick as they might have been to recognize that they, in turn, appeared almost as intransigent from yet a third standpoint. The pace at which new vistas were envisaged was too slow and clumsy for many active participants, who eventually preferred a context of their own rather than spend precious energy at a time of great ferment of ideas trying to budge the established organizations. As mentioned already, a constituency of Black scholars left the ASA in 1969 over the the representation of Africans and African-Americans in key capacities, and after raising "suspicions about the compromise settlement" (Challenor 1969: 6) that was eventually suggested. The African Heritage Studies Association was formed to promote study and debate along lines that was thought more fruitful. Comparable processes on campuses across the nation led to the institutionalization of Black, Africana and African-American Studies departments and programs.

AFRICAN STUDIES IN THE UNITED STATES

It is likely that some Black scholars who might otherwise have been in African Studies found these other contexts more stimulating and congenial during the 1970s and that there were corresponding institutional tensions. Some universities combined African and African-American Studies under the rubric of Africana Studies. On the whole, though, our institutions—including funding institutions—maintain a quite rigorous division between the two fields of study, with separate programs, degree requirements, funding criteria and so on. In theory this should not create problems because collaborative work can certainly be envisaged and organized when faculty and students share common interests. But when resources are at stake it almost certainly does create frictions. At some universities there appears to be some effort at intellectual convergence, either through particular leadership (such as Gates and Appiah at Harvard), through programmatic commitment (see the special number of *ISSUE*), or through an intellectual focus on the connections between Africa and its diaspora. In other places, scholars maintain a regional or thematic rather than diasporic definitional basis to the field; a person is a West Africanist, or a Caribbeanist, or a labor historian, rather than a specialist in Black cultural and social history.

This is a moving frontier, for intellectual, social and organizational reasons, which may find different resolutions in different universities. In an era of cost containment, some faculties may be put under pressure to merge. This is a dilemma for which there is probably no single "right answer" because the ways of doing top quality work depend on resources and commitments that will vary from place to place. But the stage is certainly set for a series of new discussions about collaboration and separate integrity across the spectrum of disciplines, programs and organizations. Given the likelihood of new external contexts for our work, it would seem useful to start thinking about these issues.

ii) Universities are under pressure to diversify the faculty, and the effort to put minority scholarships in place is just beginning to bear fruit in African Studies. Many universities can only afford one African historian. The logic is inexorable that they would prefer that one to act as an encouragement to the minority student body, as well as boost their own diversity factor, but they cannot usually declare so openly. Philip Curtin (1995) has put forward one perspective, that this constitutes ghettoization. A critique of this terminology, and its assumptions of segregation and creeping inferiority, was expressed at the Urbana conference, and is presented in the special issue of *ISSUE* (1995). One fundamental constituent of the problem is the competition for academic jobs in African history that set in about twenty years ago, and has sent at least one very well-known scholar abroad to pursue a career. No solution can be found without addressing the content of training for a job market that is so excruciatingly competitive. Most people must surely see this without us all having to "take sides," except in a single phalanx to request that the terminology be altered, and that all the implications of closure and inferiority that come with it be eliminated. The substance must be open to examination and discussion from all angles.

iii) Scholarly authority was raised in articles by Tiyambe Zeleza and Thandika Mkandawire, and is addressed intermittently in many gatherings. Zeleza tabulated the authorship of articles in five major journals from 1982-92 and found that only 17% were written by Africans (Johnson 1994:124). He urged that African scholars should simply confine their publications to Africa-based journals. Mkandawire has devoted large parts of his career to developing such publication outlets, but argues equally forcefully for the maintenance of high levels of competence in intellectual work, which he sees as having sometimes been eroded in African contexts.

These are serious and long-term issues about how and where agendas are set. In my own opinion the problems derive at least as much from the iron control of the disciplines on creditation in the American university system, and from the very competitive phase we are in, as they do from any personal or collective articulated position about the issues in question. To get a job, gain promotion and get tenure in a U.S. university, now more than ever you have to leap the disciplinary hurdles. Disciplines may be flexible about various aspects of a scholar's work if it obviously meets or surpasses the standards of artisanship (coverage, logic, empirical richness and so on). But without publication in certain key peer-review journals or reputed presses the gates are quite simply barred. It's non-negotiable and it's not resolvable through any known tactics of confrontation.

We need very urgently to think through the implications of this situation in our own contexts of work, because many of them are not unique and we need to be able to separate those that we might influence from those we cannot. First of all, no-one in the academy will change the artisanal standards except from within. But we can a) recognize the issue and take a lead in shifting criteria where they no longer make any sense, b) make spaces for work done in other ways, and c) address the contingent problems that make the situation that Zeleza identified possible in the first place. It is interesting to see that some of the concerns and dilemmas are almost identical to those raised in South-east Asian studies (Raphael 1994), including the pervasive sense that the problem actually deepened during "my" second era, when area studies participated in the disciplinary debates about theory.

Since we do now have African and African-American intellectual leadership, the lines are no longer racial. I have heard African-American colleagues argue forcefully for a position that most of us can readily share: *both* the extension of opportunity to minority categories *and* the critical importance of implementing standards in every particular case. In a situation that is as competitive as ours, they are not mutually exclusive; minority resources add both quantitatively and qualitatively to the total pool.

Beyond that, all questions of authority are bound to be a struggle. They should be, because there are real issues of the quality and the meaning of the work at stake in a time of rapid and unpredictable change. The terms of the African Heritage Studies Association's statement of purpose—"to reconstruct and present African history and cultural studies in a manner that is relevant to African peoples"- remains a challenge to be grappled with. We are well served by those who are trying to do so, as long as discussions can lead to alliances. Presenting a public image of chronic and unresolvable confrontation will only convince our administrators, to everyone's detriment, that the intellectual agendas of "reconstruction" and the constituency agendas of "relevance" can be simply distinguished and dealt with separately.

Field Research in the 1990s

I have tried to define the assets that African Studies brings to the third era of its history. They are very substantial and very valuable, and the challenge now is to make them work in new ways. The most important are a) the fieldwork training tradition, b) institutions that embody a past commitment to Africa that is presently threatened, c) experience in creating trans-Atlantic linkages, and d) a set of scholars who have made major contributions and are already pressing on frontiers that interface with international studies. All four of these assets need to be reshaped and redirected. People are already making inroads on all these points.

If there is a single point of complete agreement within the African Studies community it is the value of extended field research in Africa. Vansina's generation was able to afford as much as every other year in the field for ten years or more (see Vansina 1994). By the time Tony Waters did his dissertation research he could write: "The academic career...has a rhythm which is...incompatible with research in rural Africa. The PhD takes 9 years....

AFRICAN STUDIES IN THE UNITED STATES

This then leads to a 7 year-long fight for tenure.... The net result is that in the first 12-15 years of a promising academic career, no more than 1-2 years will be spent in Africa" (1995). Even those 1-2 years are now achieved by a select few, while everyone trained in what were accepted as "classic" field methods knows that the really valuable innovative work is done on the basis of longer and more intense research in Africa than 10% or less of one's time can possibly sustain. Our European colleagues and some of our own most productive scholars may spend up to four years on a single project. And class-time for the remaining 10-13 years is not necessarily spent in ways that enhance confidence and productivity in the field. It is a major tribute to the quality of the students in African Studies that they achieve such good work under such limiting conditions.

The situation is bad in and of itself, but also contributes in obvious ways to all the others: the anger of African colleagues about the bases for scholarly authority, the difficulty of budging the disciplines, the high rate of attrition in graduate school, the long years it takes to finish a dissertation and slow publication. To cope with relatively short stays in Africa we should be helping students to be as effective as possible during the time they do have by wedging field research into the curriculum for students from freshmen on, and teaching it as a whole toolbox of interdisciplinary skills. By the time a graduate student goes to Africa to do dissertation research they should already have done a variety of projects, both here and abroad. Even if there is money, it will take time, compromise and diplomacy in dealing with departments to come anywhere close to meeting this goal.

One benefit of a more aggressive approach to getting students to collect and work with original data from early on would be that dissertation projects could become more multidisciplinary in method, across disciplines different than the classics of anthropology and history, without over-diluting the student's level of professional competence in field research. In brief, for certain topics a student could reduce the time spent in the field, and use it in strategic combination with other methods. Africa is no longer as limited as it was in basic documentation. Remote sensing data are collected on a regular basis; there are published daily reports on the broadcast news (Foreign Broadcast Information Service, the VOA daily publication); there are various sources on the Internet; archives and libraries have collected invaluable sources in print, film and recorded media, including fieldnotes and the raw data from village agricultural studies; there are massive surveys, such as the Demographic and Health Surveys, that contain more information than the original researchers ever use. With electronic communication, totally new resources are within most scholars' reach.

An advantage of a strategic approach to fieldwork would be the new disciplinary combinations made possible. Another would be the gains in geographical coverage. At present, it's hard to imagine anyone spending the long periods of time needed for classic field research in some of the situations we read about in Africa. And yet if we do not, the entire literature on those areas and subjects will be provided by journalists. The possibility of combining careful analyses of already collected original data with a focused field component of, say, two or three months makes staying in Zaire or on the Sudan border, less completely daunting that it would otherwise be.

It is not often recognized in African Studies that the long intensive field trip has become controversial within anthropology on the grounds that it makes the linking of local and global forces quite difficult. In the mid-1980s there were some more or less powerful critiques made of the Malinowskian tradition: Llobera on its inapplicability to addressing larger political cultural dynamics in Europe, Marcus and Fischer on the need for multi-site ethnography in the era of global processes. As far as I know, anthropology has not done anything very systematic about changing training with these critiques in mind, along with the vastly changed data availability and the difficulty of the African situation. The topic bears reopening, not to abandon the unwavering commitment to field research but to adapt it to changed conditions within both academia and Africa, and to offer alternatives within courses of training.

The Civic Mandate

The organizations of African Studies are suited to stable conditions. We are faced with a different challenge at present and into the foreseeable future. In an academic situation of increased pressure, people are also faced with the need to mobilize participation in public debates "off-calendar." Those who maintain a public commitment are stretched extremely thin because there are very few organizational resources that they can tap, and little in the way of an infrastructure to designate, plan or simply react in a concerted way to events in Africa or in the U.S. The ASA cannot lobby; its Current Affairs work is as active as the board member who is responsible for it at the time; the Association of Concerned African Scholars, which worked hard on South Africa, has only partially turned around to address the rest of the continent, and it too is a volunteer enterprise; and we are not systematically linked into the Africa lobby in Washington such as TransAfrica (except the African-American membership) and the new Constituency for Africa. Our French colleagues were very active in the public debate in the wake of the Rwanda tragedy; on the whole, we were not, except for a handful of Rwanda specialists. When our members feel that the situation absolutely demands an active response they take up consultancy or put scholarship on the back burner altogether.

Political responsiveness has perhaps never been a great forte of scholars, but it was one of the guiding hopes of the area studies vision, that scholars would be a public resource in times of need for informed opinion. Junior faculty cannot possibly afford to take the time to be active in public life because the standards for professional advancement at the university—in teaching, publications and service—have become so demanding. One could see this as a recipe for quietism, especially by comparison with the past. But some people are still putting forth the effort, across the spectrum of philosophical conviction, to fulfil the civic duty of being an area studies specialist, trained and supported at the public expense (even if the amounts of money are so comparatively small). Particularly difficult personal situations are created for our African-American colleagues, for whom community involvement is an expectation. During a recent Harvard forum on "The Responsibility of the Intellectual in the Age of Crack," only Gates of all the African-American academics on the panel was able to say—and even then, only when pressed at question time—that he saw his scholarship and university service as a contribution to the community. How can anyone, and in particular junior faculty, be a scholar, maintain a personal and family life and also meet the expectations of public leadership at the same time under present conditions?

I leave this unresolved problem until last. There is no clear solution. More efficient linkage into organizations would help. Designation of points of mobilization so that we can actually fulfil one of the expectations of the area studies vision seems necessary. Junior faculty, and particularly African-Americans, probably need a sabbatical around their third or (at the latest) fourth year of service, to make sure that the necessary publications for tenure are out before the sixth year, and to thereby make it possible for them to even dream of public engagement. I hear from several quarters of the American public life that we scholars of Africa are not outspoken enough, on enough important topics. There are many ingredients to the explanation for this perception, but facing the issue is critically important over the next few years when Africa, U.S. foreign and domestic policy, and academia are all in flux at once.

6
CONCLUDING SUMMARY AND SUGGESTIONS

Why should there be support for the scholarly study of Africa?

The uniqueness of Africa has always been a matter of contention. I have heard in several different contexts the argument that if we suggest that the continent needs special programs, or different analytical concepts, then we consign it to marginality. In the new thinking about internationalization, Africa is *already* marginal. In a recent 35-page article in *The Economist* entitled "The Global Economy: War of the Worlds," Africa is listed in the first table as likely to show a mid-range growth rate over the next ten years. But in the entire far-ranging text, arguing that Third World growth is the wave of the future, it is mentioned again only once, and then as a threat: "if rich countries face any threat from the third world, it will come not from countries enjoying rapid economic growth, but from the 500m or so people, most of them in Africa, who risk being left out of the global boom" (1994:37). And the article continues without a backward glance to the startling intellectual—not to mention political and moral—challenge of a theory of global economic growth that does not even address such a massive anomaly.

Africa has always been, in fact, a "special case"—in the same way that China is a special case—even as it has shared characteristics with other regions of the world. Those originalities and common grounds have been the special concern of scholars in African Studies, and out of the struggle to understand both the differences and convergences there have emerged some striking insights into the world at large. I know this best from areas in which I have been involved. During the early 1980s several Africanist anthropologists argued that households were not unitary decision-makers as economic theory assumed. By the end of the decade, initially-skeptical economists had developed an alternative model that dealt with our observations, and were finding it applicable to completely different areas of the world: Brazil, Thailand, the Caribbean and the U.S. This is the kind of contribution we can potentially make, based on the classic methods of field research, and comparative and theoretical study.

One could add many examples: in the humanities, on the relationship between oral genres and written work; in music, on the structured thinking that produces improvisation; in demography, on concepts of the female reproductive life cycle in high fertility regimes; in the philosophy of science, on logics for conceptualizing the properties of a thing; in political science, on prebendalism, ethnicity and the dynamics of state failure; and in economics, on the links between credit and insurance in nonwestern economies. African disasters also attract scholarship that informs other world areas: on AIDS, refugees, ethnic warfare, and the character of dictatorship, for example. The "marginal" situation of Africa in the globalized world is shared by many other populations within otherwise-growing economies. We have a whole literature on the rift in our own society between those with skills adaptable to an information era and those without. From another angle, Afrocentric scholars argue the particular inspiration of Africa, and African colleagues point out how little is still known of "endogenous knowledge." There remain classical terrains of enquiry on which there are still only one or two major works, such as African theories and practices of rhetoric, moral philosophy and jurisprudence. Research on Africa, by African scholars as well as ourselves, is not just a geographical stake in an "area studies" world; it is a contribution to the understanding of global phenomena and common human experience that has made African cultures and societies "special cases."

As we all enter a new era of scholarship, where work is more tailored to specific themes and constituencies, we risk to diminish and to starve the basic research endeavor in Africa. The constituents are few, poor or over-convinced that they already have the right answers in models that come from elsewhere. Identifying themes and intellectual networks, building constituencies and responding to them is hard work. The basic assets, however, have been laid down during the past two eras, so strategic infusions in effort and resources would bring much higher returns than they cost. We have a cadre of junior people, who would be full participants in the endeavor, that is far better than any logic of the material costs and benefits available in this branch of study could possibly explain.

The community of academic scholars has been facing reduced resources since the early 1980s, so there is a great deal of experience of what works. There exist both a wide range of different expertise, and a few people who have been thinking programmatically for many years. The leadership has begun to turn over, and now includes more African-Americans, women and younger men who are ready to recognize the need for change and embrace it. These people will carry on for many more years, because they are clearly valued in their universities which have—on the whole and surprisingly—protected African Studies from the rounds of initial cuts. But they may not be replaced, for a variety of reasons that the following list of possible strategic interventions could help to counteract. All have been mentioned in the text; they are pulled out here as a summary.

AFRICAN STUDIES IN THE UNITED STATES

Linkages

The links to Africa clearly need strengthening. The most urgent and practical interventions would increase African-American student travel to Africa at early stages, and capitalize on the rising American interest in shorter-term foreign visits to help deal with the negative imagery of the safety situation in Africa. For African scholars, the greatest needs are at the junior level, where well-trained people's careers have been stalled by the sudden deterioration of conditions over the past eight years.

● *Undergraduate programs in Africa would benefit from being specialized by skill or discipline, by including a work/internship component, and by giving special attention to African-American students.*

● *Long term dissertation research needs to be protected and ensured.*

● *Faculty and scholar interchanges in most places outside of Southern Africa would benefit from working with networks, for thematic purposes, with flexible locations, rather than with institutions, for generalized purposes, on a strict partnership basis.*

● *Special attention needs to be focused on the junior faculty in Africa, such as resources to bring them to international meetings on their own topics of expertise (i.e., different from attendance at generalized meetings such as the ASA annual conference). The networks of organizations such as CODESRIA and AERC (African Economic Research Consortium) could help with identifying potential candidates.*

Training

Numbers and quality of students have been maintained both at the graduate and undergraduate level, but dissertations take far too long and the attrition level is probably quite high. There is a perceptible rising tide of dissatisfaction on the part of students and administrations with the current practice of PhD training in the core disciplines that train Africanists. Our convictions about the value of language training and field research, which are both very time-consuming, need to be realistically assessed alongside other requirements, so that they can be preserved and made more productive.

● *We should make a major effort at better preparation of students for field research: through courses, local research practicums and innovative language teaching.*

AFRICAN STUDIES IN THE UNITED STATES

• *We should explore and encourage the combination of shorter-term field research with analysis of databases (not only quantitative and scientific data, but including media reports and other modern textual sources).*

We have no solid data on the African-American student body in African Studies. Their eligibility for minority fellowships at the entry level at almost all institutions protects them from the statistically-expectable elimination (due to their numbers in the pool) that could result when there are so few entering students, as there are in most of our disciplines. The same may not be true for field research funds which have become very scarce. We may be wasting at the research stage some of the talent and training that has been cultivated at the coursework stage.

• *It is worth studying the participation of African-American students in field research, with a view to making sure that the current extremely tight budgets, with very limited targeted programs, do not effectively discourage or eliminate them.*

Just as African Studies moved from graduate to undergraduate teaching in the 1970s, we now have to incorporate professional schools and students from programs other than the classic core, including the scientific disciplines engaged with environmental, health and population issues.

• *We need to increase a presence in the professional schools and build further on collaboration with the sciences.*

The disciplines have been both a strength and the Achilles heel of the effort to internationalize the curriculum. It is they, and not area studies, that have blocked the study of the rest of the world. Economics has been particularly powerful in this regard. The only solid claim to representation that African Studies has within the disciplines is intellectual originality, not a generalized need to know about the world. We will continue to survive on this basis as in the past, but not necessarily with as strong a capacity as is needed to address all the agendas and to ensure context-sensitivity in global studies.

• *Interdisciplinearity needs reconfirming, in course work and research, because otherwise efforts to internationalize will again be thwarted, regardless of the names of programs.*

• *Different combinations of disciplinary studies than we have had in the past need to be encouraged.*

There is a cadre of junior-level faculty (or just tenured), who have a good grip on both quantitative and other methods. There are no junior faculty awards in our field (as far as I know), unlike in the sciences where they seem to abound, and no ways of targeting resources to them for collaborative and programmatic work.

86

AFRICAN STUDIES IN THE UNITED STATES

● *Some strategic funding or recognition award could be offered to junior faculty who bridge the disciplines in new ways: to offer recognition and to use to help organize networks around key issues in current studies.*

Organizations

For the moment, the organizations which ensure our existence continue to give support, although at a steadily eroding level, with the exception of some of the support for development economics that almost certainly accounts for the majority of discretionary funding available for research on the continent. Only certain segments of the funding picture are designated for Africa, and these are primarily for South Africa; the Foundations, for example, are mainly thematic in interest.

● *We have to relate to more of these organizations, and compete along thematic lines. The pervasive image of Africa as marginal is going to create barriers to convincing funders of the general relevance of African Studies but there's no alternative, and the international/global thrust offers a good forum.*

If I am correct that we are moving towards more constituency-oriented research, then the African Studies community will need to be more active in defining and negotiating what needs to be done. There is every sign that scholars are, in fact, being consulted and brought into discussion of Africa to a greater degree than was the case in the 1980s, which creates tremendous time pressures in the context of university demands. Some of our colleagues are serving in so many capacities—from public education about Rwanda to brainstorming about potential innovations in methods teaching and addressing multiculturalism and minority politics on campus—that it's hard to imagine how they still produce scholarship (which they do). Some of the impression of diffuseness in the field is strictly a function of the localistic "brush-fire" approach to "matters arising."

● *There need to be something like one-semester "public service leaves" for some senior faculty members, explicitly to engage with formulation of approaches to the key programmatic problems that face us all.*

The Joint Committee on African Studies of the Social Science Research Council and American Council of Learned Societies has the confidence of the African Studies community and well represents our network mode of organization. At critical moments it has provided leadership for the field as a whole. The committee on Africa remains a single committee after the SSRC reorganization, but with a very limited fellowship budget.

● *The committee needs a budget and a mandate for developing an orientation for the next few years (a "mission statement") towards reconfiguring its activities.*

In the spirit of building on assets that already exist, the differing bases of African Studies at different universities needs embracing as a strength. The response to the current round of proposals indicates great enthusiasm for opportunities to build on unique local assets such as a museum collection, library, or links to what is probably the largest epidemiology center in the world (the CDC in Atlanta).

● *A regular competition for small planning grants in African Studies would offer the seed money for the local initiatives that will become more important in the next era.*

Debates

We are already engaged in many relevant debates about the future. They are not as coordinated as they could be, but the field is not polarized into factions. In fact, the new generation of senior faculty comprises very long term friendship and collegial networks across all the classic fault-lines of our society. We have recognized leadership amongst African, African-American and white scholars from various countries, and they come with a huge fund of experience in collaboration and frank discussion of sensitive issues. Most of what I know about the field at large comes from them and they have responded with great interest to my requests for information.

● *It could be useful to go a large step farther than an individual report, to organize a round of collective discussion, possibly using the report as a basis. People have suggested this to me.*

We have the Internet, but probably not the right kind of organizations to respond to the exigencies of the moment that are presented to us on the screen and in the press.

● *We need to devise better ways, under the present circumstances, to fulfill the civic function that area studies was supposed to take on, namely engaging with the public on the issues affecting the area of the world in which we work.*

AFRICAN STUDIES IN THE UNITED STATES

REFERENCES CITED

Articles

Bay, Edna
  1991. "African Studies Association." In National Council of Area Studies, *Prospects for Faculty in Area Studies*, 1-18.

Challenor, Herschelle Sullivan
  1969 "No Longer at Ease: Confrontation at the 12th Anual African Studies Association Meeting in Montreal." *Africa Today* 16(5 and 6): 4-7.

Chege, Michael
  1994. "What's Right with Africa?" *Current History*, 93(583):193-197.

Collier, Paul
  1994. "Africa and the Study of Economics." In Bates, Robert H., V.Y. Mudimbe and Jean O'Barr (eds.) *Africa and the Disciplines: The Contributions of Research in Africa to the Social Sciences and Humanities.* Chicago: University of Chicago Press, 58-82.

Curtin, Philip D.
  1995. "Ghettoizing African History." *The Chronicle of Higher Education*, March 3:A44.

Economist, The
  1994. "The Global Economy: War of the Worlds." October 1:3-38.

Heginbotham, Stanley J.
  1994. "Rethinking International Scholarship: The challenge of transition from the cold war era." *Items*: Social Science Research Council 48(2,3): 33-40.

Johnson, David
  1994. "Reconstructing The Study and Meaning of Africa." *South Asia Bulletin*, 14(1): 122-125.

Kaplan, Robert D.
  1994. "The Coming Anarchy." *Atlantic Monthly*, 273(2): 487-506.

Lauer, Joseph J.
  1989. "Geography of African Studies: Regional and National Emphases in Dissertation and Other Research." In   Julian W. Witherell (ed.) *Africana Resources and Collections. Three Decades of Development and Achievement. A Festschrift in Honor of Hans Panofsky.* Metuchen, N.J.: The Scarecrow Press, 178-193.

AFRICAN STUDIES IN THE UNITED STATES

Mamdani, Mahmood
1990. "A Glimpse at African Studies, Made in USA." *CODESRIA Bulletin*, 2:7-11.

Mkandawire, Thandika
1993. "Problems and prospects of social sciences in Africa." *International Social Sciences Journal*, 135: 130-140.

Owomoyela, Oyekan
1994. "With Friends like These...A Critique of Pervasive Anti-Africanisms in Current African Studies Epistemology and Methodology." *African Studies Review*, 37(3): 77-101.

Plattner, Stuart; Gary Aronson and Benjamin Abellera
1993. "Commentary - Recent Trends in Funding Anthropological Research at the National Science Foundation." *Human Organization*, 52(1): 110-114.

Plattner, Stuart; Linda Hamilton, and Marilyn Madden
1987. "The Funding of Research in Social-Cultural Anthropology at the National Science Foundation." *American Anthropologist*, 89: 853-866.

Plattner, Stuart and Christopher McIntyre
1991. "Commentary - The Funding of Dissertation Research in Anthropology at the National Science Foundation." *Human Organization*, 50(2): 203-208.

Raphael, Vicente L.
1994. "The Culture of Area Studies in the United States." *Social Text*, 91-111.

Richburg, Keith B.
1995. "Continental Divide." *The Washington Post Magazine*, March 26, 17-25.

Robinson, Pearl T.
1990. "On Paradigms and Political Silence." *CODESRIA Bulletin*, 4:7.

Rowe, Cyprian Lamar
1970 "Crisis in African Studies: The Birth of the African Heritage Studies Association." Buffalo N.Y.: Black Academy Press.

Sanders, Rickie
1993. "The Last Decade: A Content Analysis of the African Studies Review, 1982-91." *African Studies Review*, 36(1): 115-126.

Szanton, David
1991. "Shaping the Course of Area Studies." The dissertation research awards. *Items*: Social Science Research Council, 45(2/3): 26-31, plus appendix.

Waters, Tony
1995. "Africanists and the Challenge of the Mission Veranda." *ISSUE*.

Reports and Books

Bates, Robert H., V.Y. Mudimbe and Jean O'Barr (eds.)
1993. *Africa and the Disciplines: The Contributions of Research in Africa to the Social Sciences and Humanities*. Chicago: University of Chicago Press.
Bowen, William, and Neil Rudenstine
1992. *In Pursuit of the PhD*. Princeton, N.J.: Princeton University Press.
Center for International Education, Department of Education
1994. "Title VI FLAS Fellowship Awards, 1988-91." Memorandum. Washington, D.C.: U.S. Department of Education 1-19. Institute of International Education Source Material.
1994. "National Security Education Program: IIE 1994-1995 Undergraduate Scholarship Summary Report." Institute of International Education Source Material, May: 1-8.
Guyer, Jane I.
1995. *Money Matters: Instability, Values and Social Payments in the Modern History of West African Communities*. Portsmouth NH: Heinemann.
Hamilton, Ruth Simms and Tony Hodges
1987. "African Affairs Institutions and Public Education in the United States." A Report to the Ford Foundation: 1-179.
Joint Committee on African Studies of the American Council of Learned Societies and Social Science Research Council
1992. "Preliminary Report on Assessment of Funding and Internship Opportunities for Social Science Graduate Students Doing Research on Health and Agriculture in Africa," 1-3.
1993. "Africa Program: IDRF Survey Summary [Draft]," 1-21.
Lambert, Richard D.
1986. *Points of Leverage. An Agenda for a National Foundation of International Studies*. New York: Social Science Research Council.
MacGaffey, Janet.
1991. *The Real Economy of Zaire: The Contributions of Smuggling and other Unofficial Activities to National Wealth*. Philadelphia, PA: University of Pennsylvania Press.
National Council for Area Studies Associations
1991. "Prospects for Faculty in Area Studies." Stanford, CA.
National Security Education Board
1994. "Charter of the National Security Education Board." 1-4.

1994. "Grants to Institutions of Higher Education: Preliminary Guidelines for 1994-95 Pilot Grants Program." 1-11.
Social Science Research Council
1992. "Assessment of Funding and Internship Possibilities for Graduate Students Doing Research on Health and Agriculture in Africa."
1994. "Strengthening and Restructuring the Core International Programs:: Recommendations of the SSRC International Program Staff Group [Discussion Draft]." 1-29.
Tripp, Aili Marie
1991. "Some Thoughts on the Funding of International Exchanges." The MacArthur Foundation, Program on Peace and International Cooperation.
Watts, Michael
1993. "Capacity Through Competition: An Evaluation of the Rockefeller Foundation African Dissertation Internship Awards (ADIA) Program 1987-1992."
Vansina, Jan
1994. *Living with Africa*. Madison WI; University of Wisconsin Press.
Wiley, David
1993. "Some New Bearings for the National Security Education Program in 1993-94." Michigan State University, 1-10.
1993. "Comments for SSRC Workshop on International Research and Training." Michigan State University, 1-10.
1994 Summary. Academy for Educational Development. 1-6.
Williams, Cynthia
1993. "Trends in Funding for International Programs at U.S. Universities." University of Wisconsin-Madison.

Documents
Center for International Education, Department of Education
Proposals to be Designated as a Comprehensive National Resource Center in African Language and Area Studies for the Title VI Foreign Language and Area Studies Fellowship and Summer Intensive Language Fellowships for the period August 15th 1994-August 14th 1997.
All proposals read.
USIA Fulbright Review Committee
1994 Second Draft.
National Security Education Program

AFRICAN STUDIES IN THE UNITED STATES

Various fliers, letters, ASA and AASP motions.

People Consulted
USAID
   Cristina Mossi, Info*Structure* International
   Hugh   Maney,   Management   Information   Systems   Specialist,
      AFR/ONI/TPPI.
   Curt Reintsma, Division Chief for Agriculture, Natural Resources, and
      Private Sector Development, AFR/SD/PSGE
   Diane Russell

Scholars
   James McCann, Director, Boston University African Studies Center
   Frederick Cooper, Department of History, University of Michigan
   Robert Price, David Leonard, and Martha Savaadra, Stanford-Berkeley
      African Studies
   Kristin Mann, Director, African Studies, Emory University
   Robert Cummings, Chair, Department of African Studies, Howard
      University
   Catharine Newbury, Department of Political Science, UNC Chapel Hill
   Achille Mbembe, Department of History, University of Pennsylvania
   Sandra Barnes, Director, African Studies, University of Pennsylvania
   William Martin and Michael West, University of Illinois-Urbana
   Gwendolyn Mikell, Department of Sociology, Georgetown University
   Michael Watts, Director of International Studies, University of California-
      Berkeley
   David Szanton, International Studies, University of California-Berkeley
   Herschelle Challenor, International Affairs, Clark-Atlanta University

Organizational Officers
   Barbara Bianco, Social Science Research Council
   Priscilla Stone, Social Science Research Council
   Jane Martin, The African-American Institute
   Joseph Lauer, Africa Collection, Michigan State University

Others who have influenced on my thinking about the issues in this report on
previous occasions include:
   Sara Berry, Sally Moore, Eileen Julien, Richard Joseph, Pearl Robinson,
   and members of the JCAS, SSRC/ACLS, 1981-6.

APPENDIXES

AFRICAN STUDIES IN THE UNITED STATES

Appendix I: Letter sent to African Studies Training Programs

February 16, 1995
Dear _____:

   I am writing to ask you, as the head of an African Studies program that is affiliated with the AASP, for some observations on the conditions of training. The Ford Foundation has asked me to review the current state of African Studies in the U.S. The sense is that the ground is shifting and that the next generation of scholars is being recruited and trained in a new context and perhaps in new ways.

   Having reviewed data on dissertations, fellowships, Title VI and so on, over time, I think that there have indeed been different cohorts: with different guiding intellectual emphases, differing composition and different structures of support at each stage of their training. But I am inferring these patterns from trends in the data, plus my own experience of different departments, centers and committees, over the years. I would like to have more confidence that I can read the intellectual, organizational and experiential realities accurately, including for places I don't know first hand. In particular, there may be emerging issues with a newest cohort of students, for which no data have been compiled at all. It would be a great enrichment of our knowledge to have as clear a view of the incoming students as we can glean of the outgoing PhDs.

   The following questions address issues for which there are no systematic data sources but which are critically important for projecting future training. If you have any data already generated for your own program it would be very helpful for me to see them. If not, I would be grateful for your ideas and impressions. I have kept it short. I don't intend this to be a large imposition on your time. In fact, be selective if you wish. I am looking for insights, not necessarily figures.

a) How would you characterize undergraduate interests in courses of study on Africa?

b) Who is choosing to take advanced training in African Studies (since, say, 1990), and do they differ from earlier cohorts in either their experience in Africa (Peace Corps, semester abroad, work) or their career plans (academia, NGOs, government)? Do the numbers of applicants seem to be stable? How would you characterize the recruitment and composition of the new class for last year?

c) Is the university support system for incoming (and up to pre-ABD) students changing, and hence their financial situation? If you know anything about indebtedness, do describe it. If there are special resources for minority or African students, please mention them.

d) Are there particular points of attrition in the graduate career, where good students are lost or delayed?

e) What would you identify as the particular weaknesses or challenges of graduate training at the moment?

Since I need to finish the report by April 1 it would be very helpful if you could send an answer by March 13. This will give me a chance to synthesize the information from all AASP members. Thank you in advance for your input. I undertake to keep all comments in confidence, with respect both to institution and author.

Yours sincerely,

Jane I. Guyer
Director

AFRICAN STUDIES IN THE UNITED STATES

Appendix II: Responses to letter sent to African Studies Training Programs

I requested information and observations from the directors of all the teaching programs that are current members of the Association of African Studies Programs (approximately 70 institutions). The questions focused on a) undergraduate interest, b) graduate recruitment, c) graduate support, d) points of attrition in graduate training, and e) weaknesses and challenges of graduate training (see Appendix A). To compose their reply some centers asked the entire faculty to contribute to a single report; in other cases I received letters from several different individuals at the same institution; in a few, the letter represented the expert view of the director.

I received answers from the 19 institutions listed below, and discussed the same issues in person with senior faculty from four more.

    University of Illinois at Urbana-Champaign
    University of Wisconsin-Madison
    Duke University
    Truman College [one of the City Colleges of Chicago]
    University of Richmond
    Boston University
    Emory University
    Purdue University (African American Studies and Research Center)
    California State University, San Bernardino
    University of California-Los Angeles
    University of California-Berkeley
    Ohio University
    University of Iowa
    Swarthmore College
    University of Florida-Gainesville
    St. Lawrence University
    Washington University-St. Louis
    University of Pennsylvania
    University of Virginia
Discussions without written response:
    Stanford University (Richard Roberts)
    Howard University (Robert Cummings)
    University of Michigan-Ann Arbor (Frederick Cooper)
    Northwestern (Akbar Virmani and faculty).

SELECTED COMMENTS
a) Undergraduate Interest

"Undergraduate interest is strong and growing...consistently at full enrollment.... Interest is especially strong among African-American students."

"Undergraduate interest in courses of study on Africa remains high."

"In the last five years or so, there seems to have been an interest in the enrollment of African-American students, with continuing interest by other students as well.... Our courses in the past few years are typically 30-60% African American."

"My own opinion is that there is relatively little undergrad. interest in African courses, though individual courses do OK in enrollment, usually because of the reputation of the instructor rather than the subject matter *per se*. We have about 1,000 African-American students here but they don't appear to be particularly drawn to African classes.... Virtually all our foreign students, who pay high fees, come from the Far East and enroll mostly in classes in the business school."

Demand for upper division courses on Africa has grown, although "This is more an indication of the high demand for the upper division level of course than of interest in its content...there are as many students in classes who are genuinely interested in Africa as there were twenty years ago. However, they are thrown in with others who have less inherent interest."

"Undergraduate interests in Africa are growing slowly.... I would say 10-15% of the students have been African-American."

"Responses ranged from 'fairly constant' to 'extremely high' interest."

"[Undergraduate] interest may be somewhat stronger now than in the past."

"'Bad news' about Africa does not have a discouraging effect on enrollment."

"I have noticed that black students on campus have expressed a great deal of interest in things African in recent years.... Many, however, still want courses that are intensely Afrocentric and few of our African American students have shown much interest in the problems of modern Africa. This will change, but slowly."

"...courses specifically on Africa seem to fill up."

b) Recruitment of Graduate Students and the Nature of Training:

"...we have seen increasing interest, but no clear trend in who the students are.

We always have a mix of backgrounds and ultimate objectives."

"...we do not have as many African students as in the past."

"Students come to study with prominent Africanists."

"...the most salient fact of the past decade...is the polycentric geography of graduate programs.... A major difference in the training is that the new programs have little of the old strengths in language, and to some degree library resources."

"...the tendency is for our students to come from places that have strong undergraduate programs in development studies, African Studies, or other relevant disciplines."

"Things have not changed much since...the late 70s and early 80s! The grad. students tend to be either RPCVs [returned Peace Corps volunteers] or Africans. A few are African-Americans who are coming into the field for the first time at the graduate level."

"...they are attracting more minorities, but minority students tend to have no previous experience in Africa...students tend to be younger than they were years ago, but still of high quality."

"...former Peace Corps experience is very important, although some come directly out of undergrad. studies."

"The number of applicants with an interest specifically in Africa has been low, but stable, over the last 15 years."

"We are getting a core of much more high powered students than, say, 6-8 years ago."

c) Graduate Support

"University support is strongest for minority students."

"We Africanists are trying to take advantage of...our minority support program.... These competitions are open to anyone, though, and there is nothing earmarked for Africanists."

"There are University-wide resources for graduate students, for minority students, but as always these are severely limited and are not necessarily funneled into African programs."

"The Rockefeller dissertation program for African students has been an enormous help... (T)he pre-dissertation awards ...have grown in importance. Students are much better prepared with institutional sponsorship, field site, etc., than a generation ago."

"If one is admitted here there are four years of funding. There are 2 special fellowship competitions, university-wide —one for minority students..."

"Fellowship opportunities are fewer than they were twenty years ago, and the amount of money available is less.... (T)he rate of PhD production per year has dropped dramatically [and probably has] to do with attrition due to the opportunity costs of pursuing the African Studies PhD.... Fewer and fewer are African Americans.... There are fellowships for minorities, but they carry the requirement of a reciprocal commitment of two year fellowship support from the receiving department...the tendency is for departments not to participate in this program.... We desperately need some independent resources for the recruitment and retention of our students."

"Numbers of applicants are stable, but acceptances have declined because we have little financial support to offer...First year students

rarely get support. Large numbers work on or off campus in menial jobs."
"As for indebtedness, the horror story that sticks in my mind [is about the student who] now has a great job...but is in a terrible hole [financially]."
"We are faced with the prospect of withdrawal of tuition waivers for some graduate students, which could affect our recruitment.... (We) have fellowships to attract minority students."
"The university's support for graduate students has not changed yet. But there is a chance that the funds for teaching assistants will decline soon.... There are specific resources for minority students on campus, but not for African students.... (But note) the upcoming anti-affirmative action initiative."
"Competition for funding is up, particularly among minorities this year, and it is heart-breaking because we do not have the resources to attract and then support them.... Some departments are better off; others not so."
"Minority fellowships allow us to keep the quality up, by allowing admission of a larger highly qualified class."

d) Points of Attrition

"Delays usually strike between coursework and fieldwork, usually due to funding."
"There is always something of a hiatus between classroom work and dissertation writing, but in most cases student determination provides necessary bridges."
"The most difficult phase to fund is the write-up."
"...the available programs to apply to for write-up money are very few."
"Students are being slowed down at the dissertation level. The cost and logistics involved with getting to the field with limited resources and coming back to write up without university support dramatically slows down the time to degree [completion], and in some cases leads to attrition."
In Agriculture "employment prospects looked poor, because ABD students who return from fieldwork are very slow in writing up dissertations because they must take time-consuming jobs to support themselves. This delay limits their chances in the current job market."
"Students are generally lost to Africa, not the university. Consideration of career opportunities and likely support for dissertation research encourages people to pursue work in world areas other than Africa."
"Good students are delayed because of i) lack of full funding which means they have to work part-time or ii) demands of field work which tend to lengthen time after doctoral exams and completion of dissertation."

e) Weaknesses and Challenges

"...Maintaining relevance as social, economic, financial, and political conditions in the US and Africa change."

The need for "periodic regeneration (that is) felt by all programs."

"...to incorporate more comparative approaches."

"...to help our students prepare for research in terms of language skills."

"...we are not doing a good job—in part because of the resource problem—at addressing the poor representation of African Americans in the current cohort of Africanists in doctoral programs. Surely opportunity costs serve as a deterrent that should not be minimized. But, there also seems not to be the will on the part of the African Studies community to forthrightly address the problem. We need a national, prestigious fellowship program for African Studies...which is targeted at this underrepresented group."

"The problem is trying to turn this fascination [with Africa] into work and careers.... Another weakness I see is the old problem of trying to get faculty to work across disciplinary boundaries."

"Fieldwork has long been a requirement for graduate students in African Studies. All informants cite changing conditions as problematic and different from the problems encountered 10-15 years ago. Massive health risks and risks to personal safety must be confronted. These, in addition to the financial outlay, make the time spent in fieldwork less than it was in the past, while faculty assert that actually more language training and longer time in the field is needed than in the past.... No one wishes to eliminate fieldwork, but consensus is that this aspect of graduate training needs serious reassessment. Post-doctoral work seems desirable to gain the depth of training needed for university scholars in most fields."

"Student morale seems low...though improving over the past few years. Academically, absorption in introspection has taken a high toll on student motivation and left them short of basic training in background, theory and method."

"(P)articular weaknesses...can be attributed to the swing toward anti-intellectual isolationism in D.C. ...."

"(T)he biggest challenge is to convince the intellectual 'gatekeepers' in our respective disciplines to continue seeing the value of area studies. Internationalization of the curricula makes little sense if area studies are not strengthened, but not all understand that."

"The challenge now is funding for field research."

"Challenges: i) reconfigurating graduate training to take into account global contexts and non-regional comparisons and insights; ii) recruiting top students among all groups including, especially, minority groups; iii) funding graduate students; iv) re-problematizing research so as to transcend essentializing discourse, over-simplification, and other modernist entanglements; and v) finding ways to rethink how students are mentored and brought into professional relationships with more senior scholars."